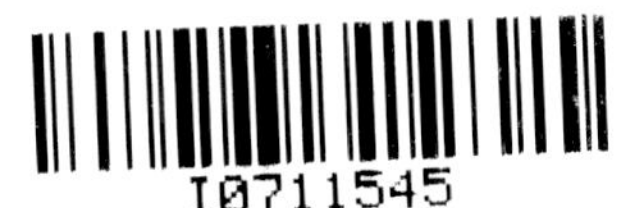

This book

belongs to

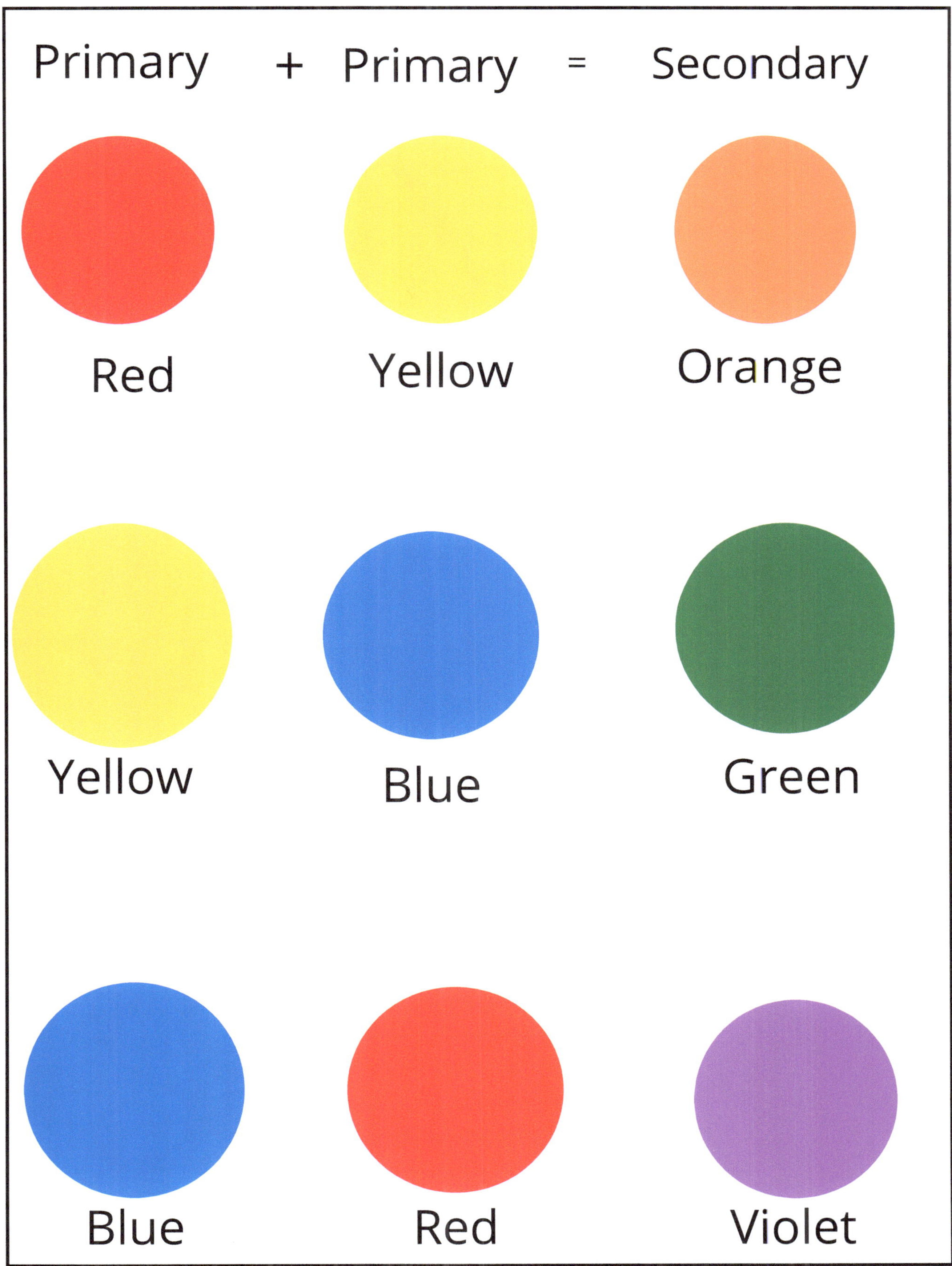

Primary + Primary = Secondary
Red
Yellow
Orange
Yellow
Blue
Green
Blue
Red
Violet

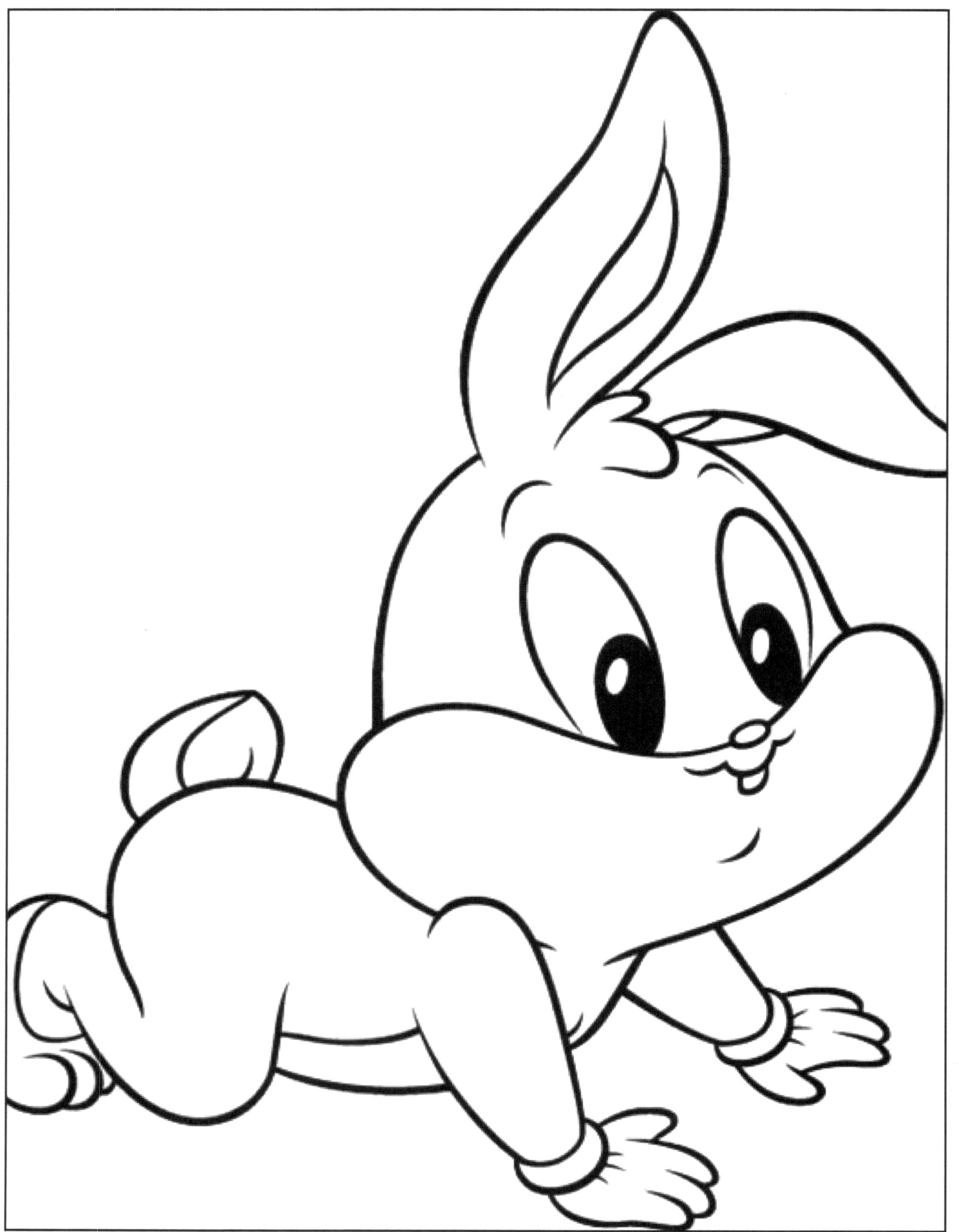

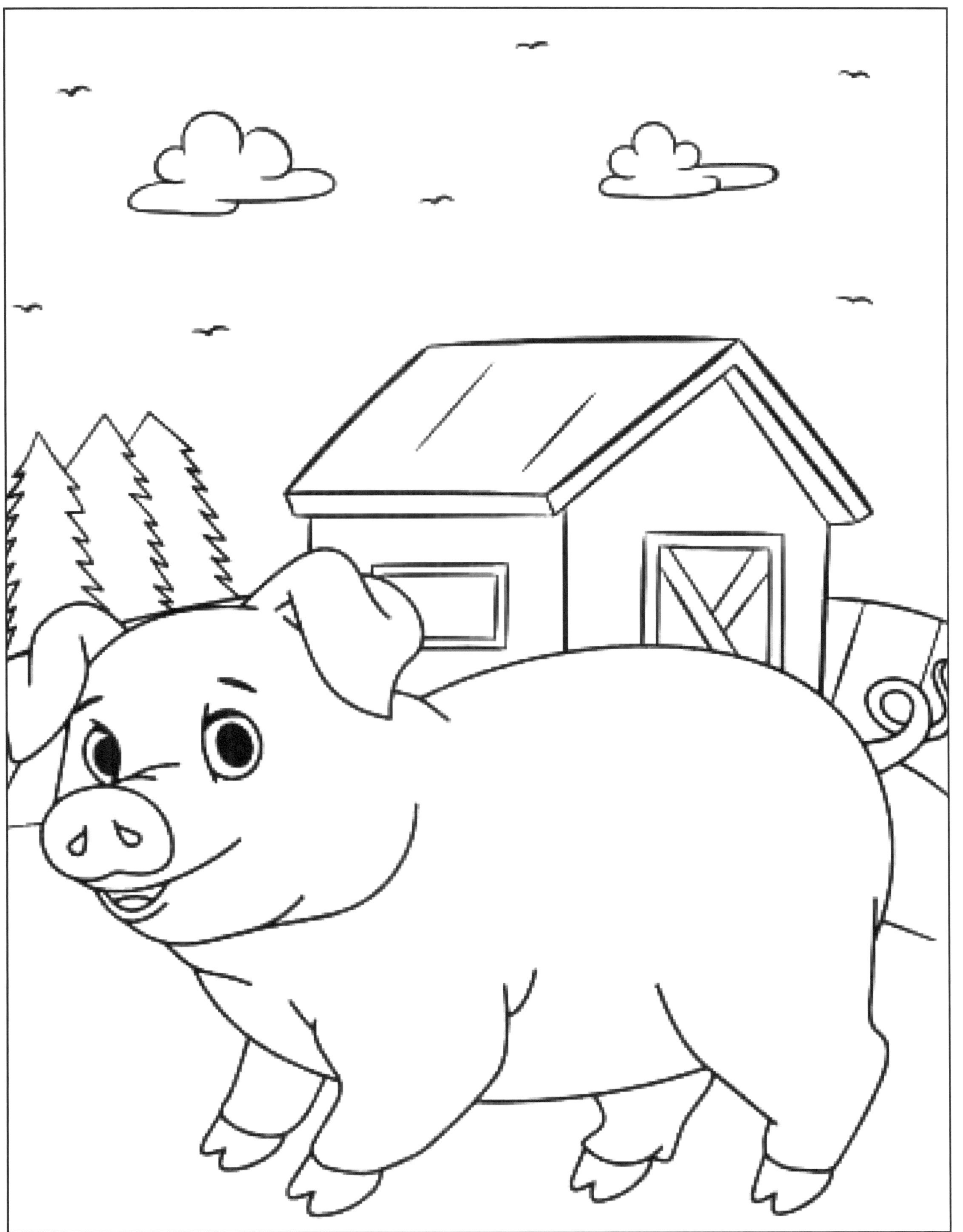

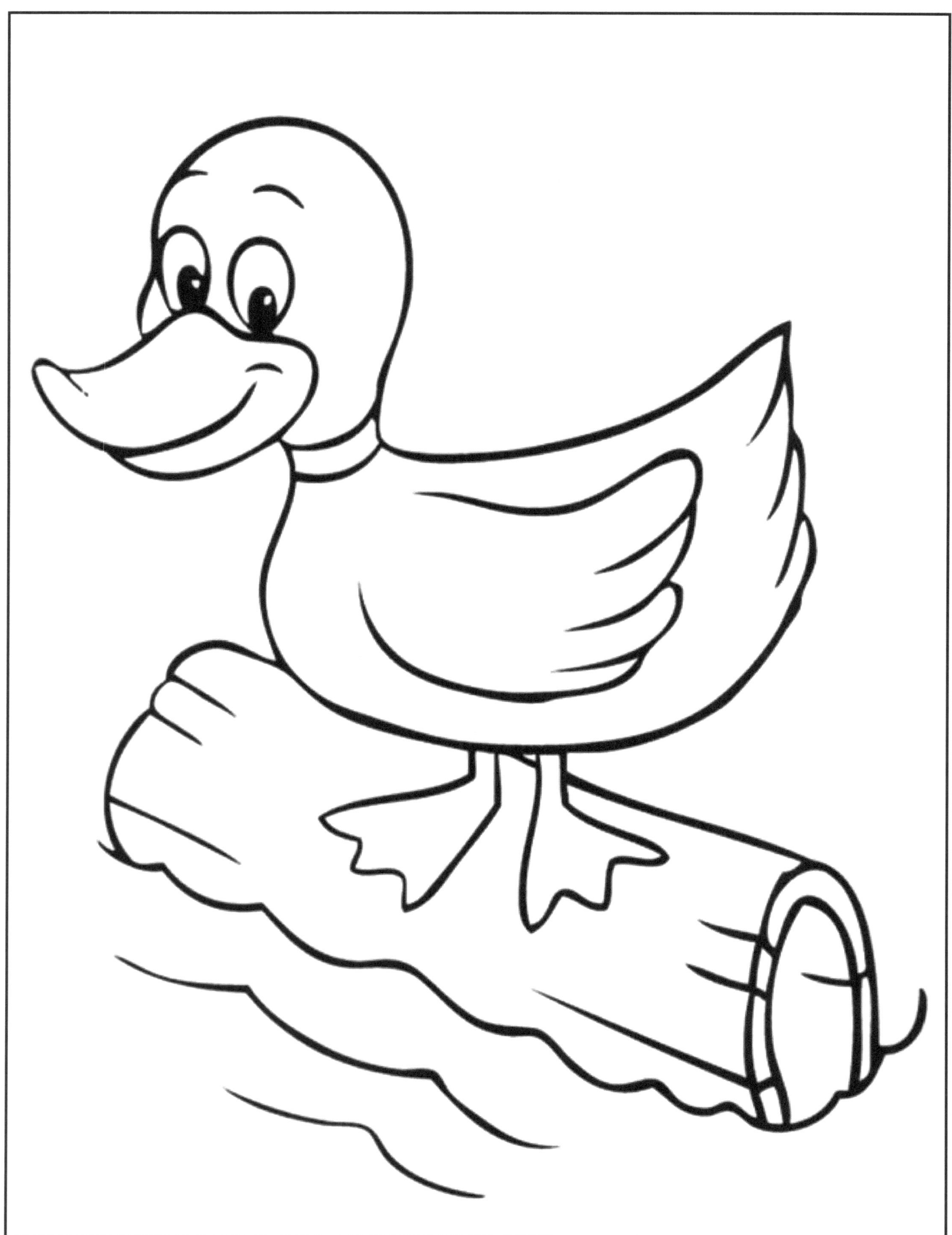

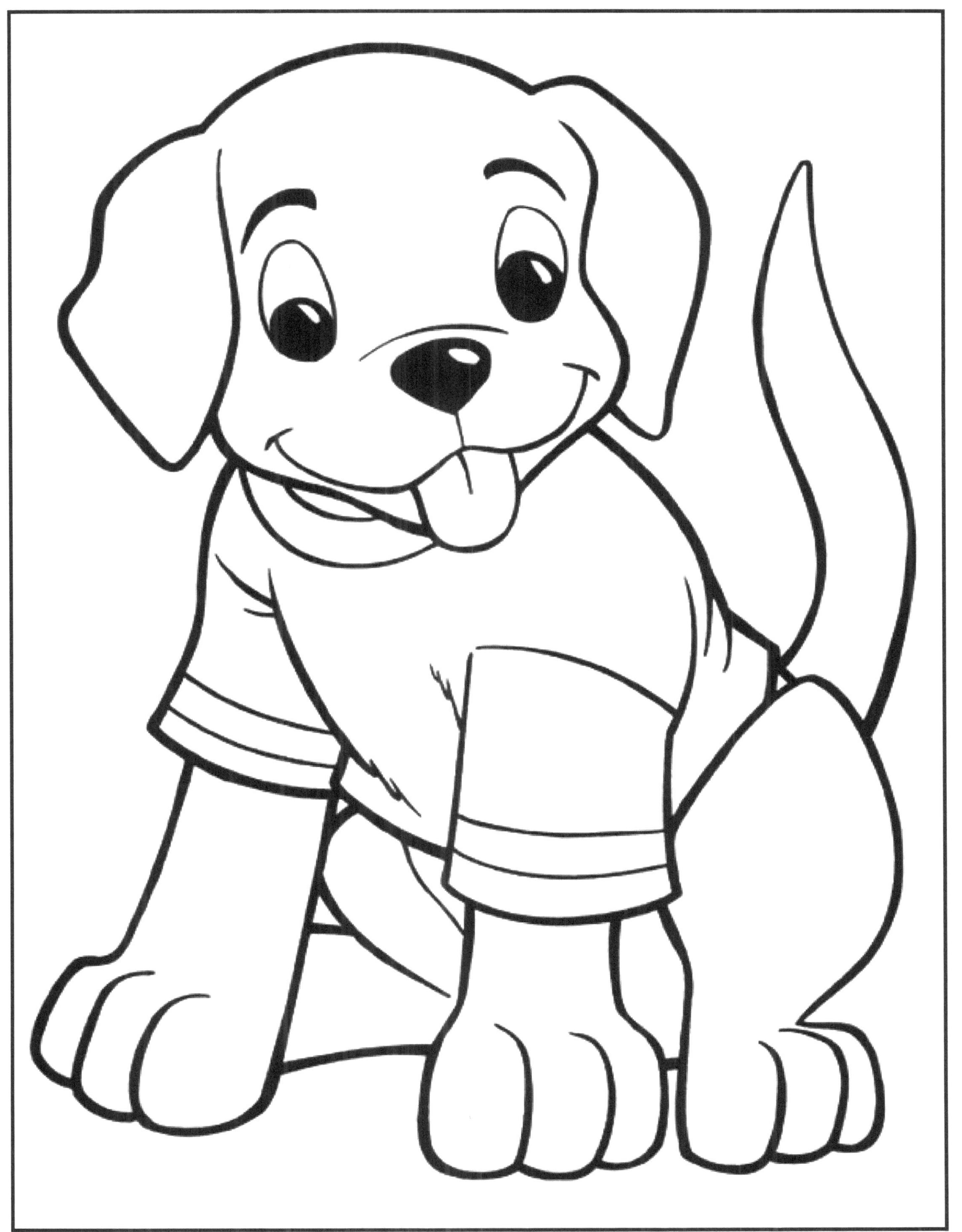

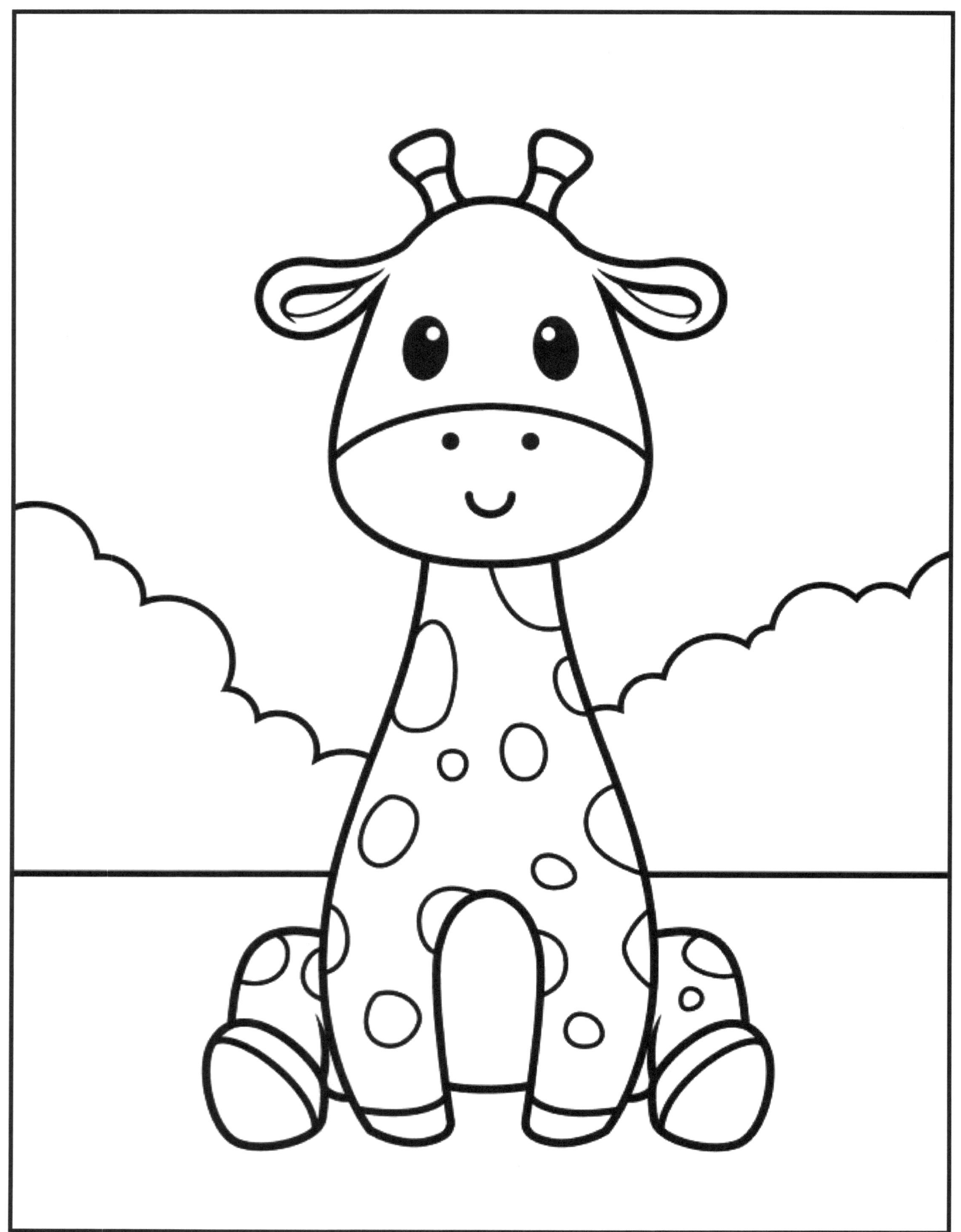

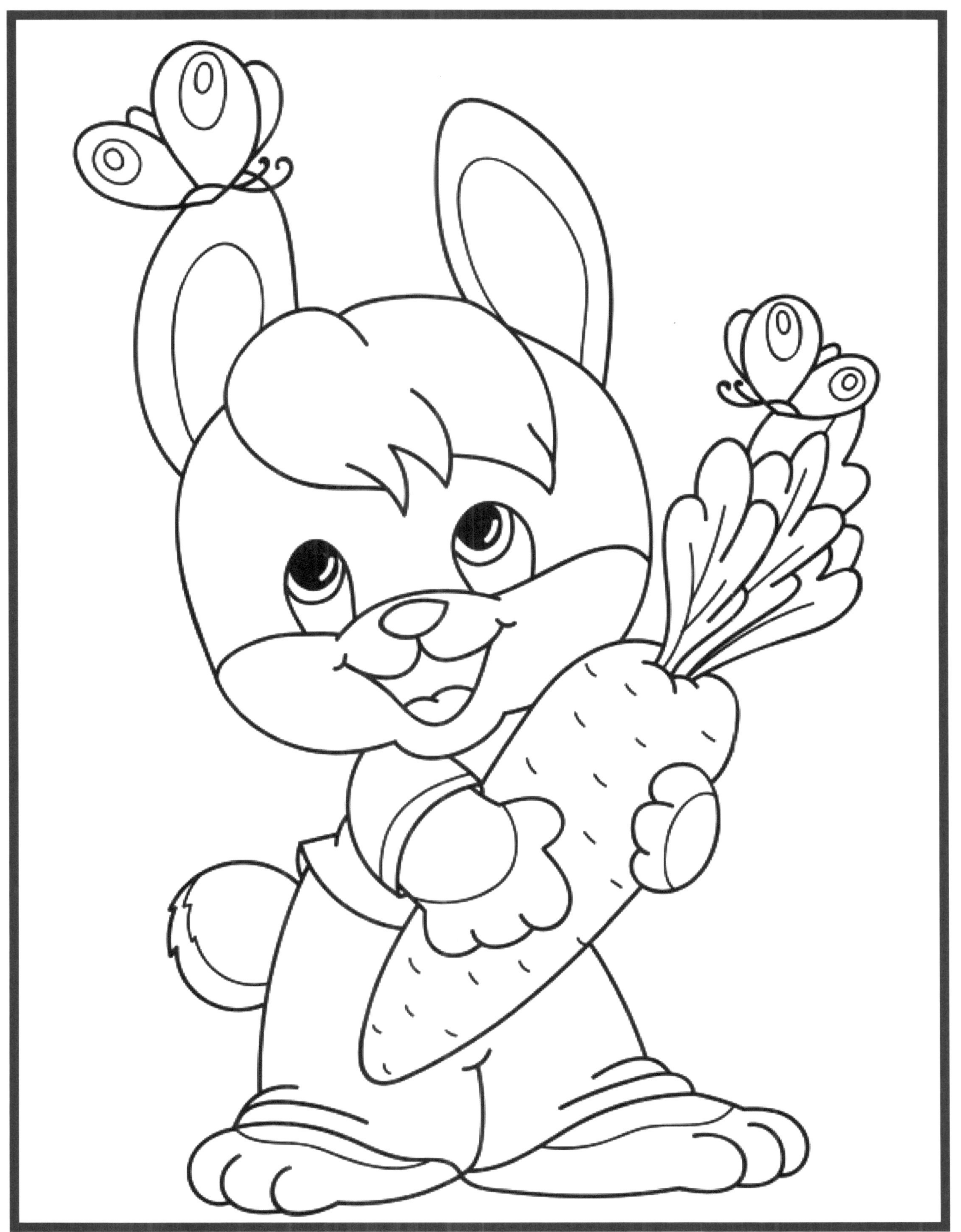

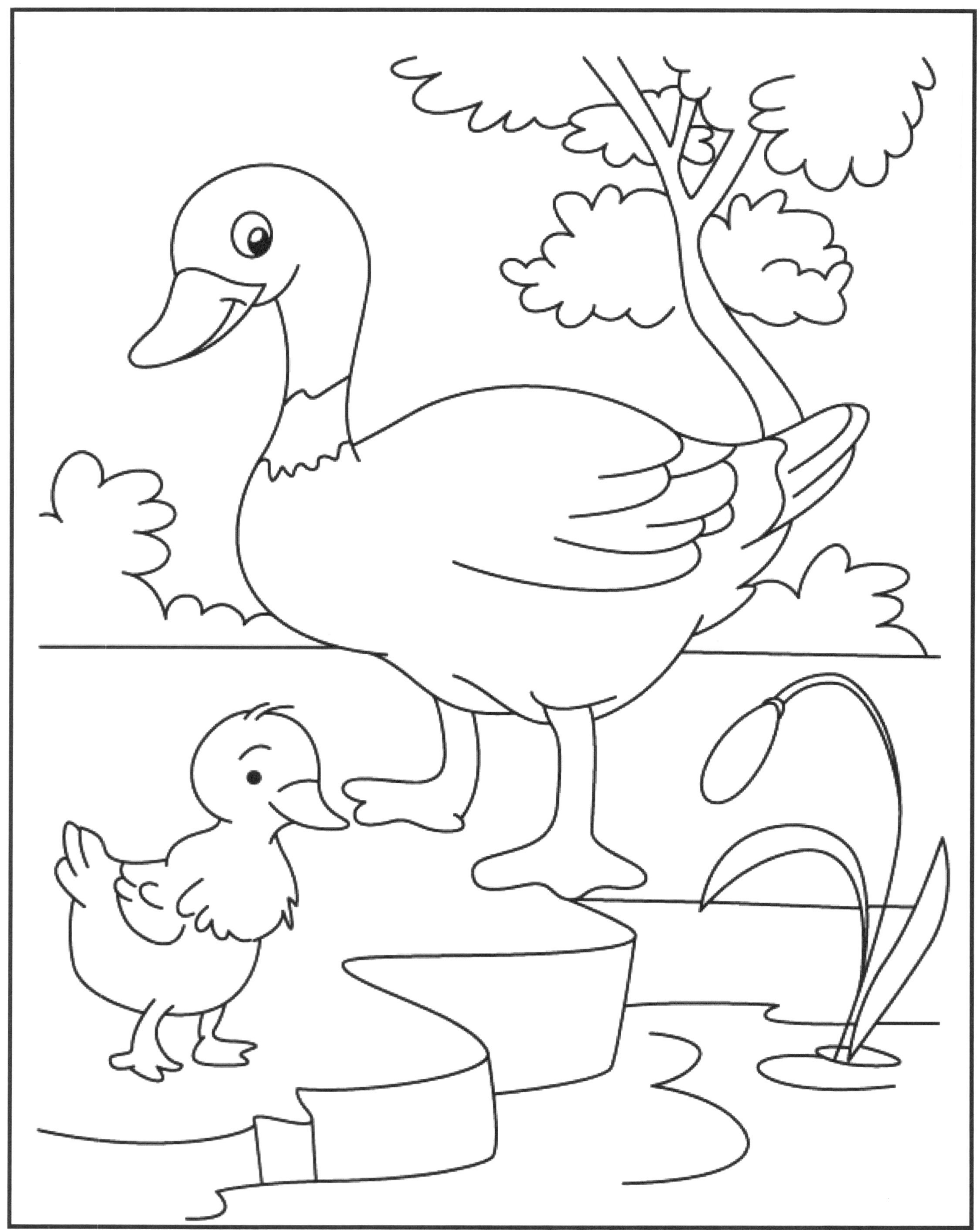

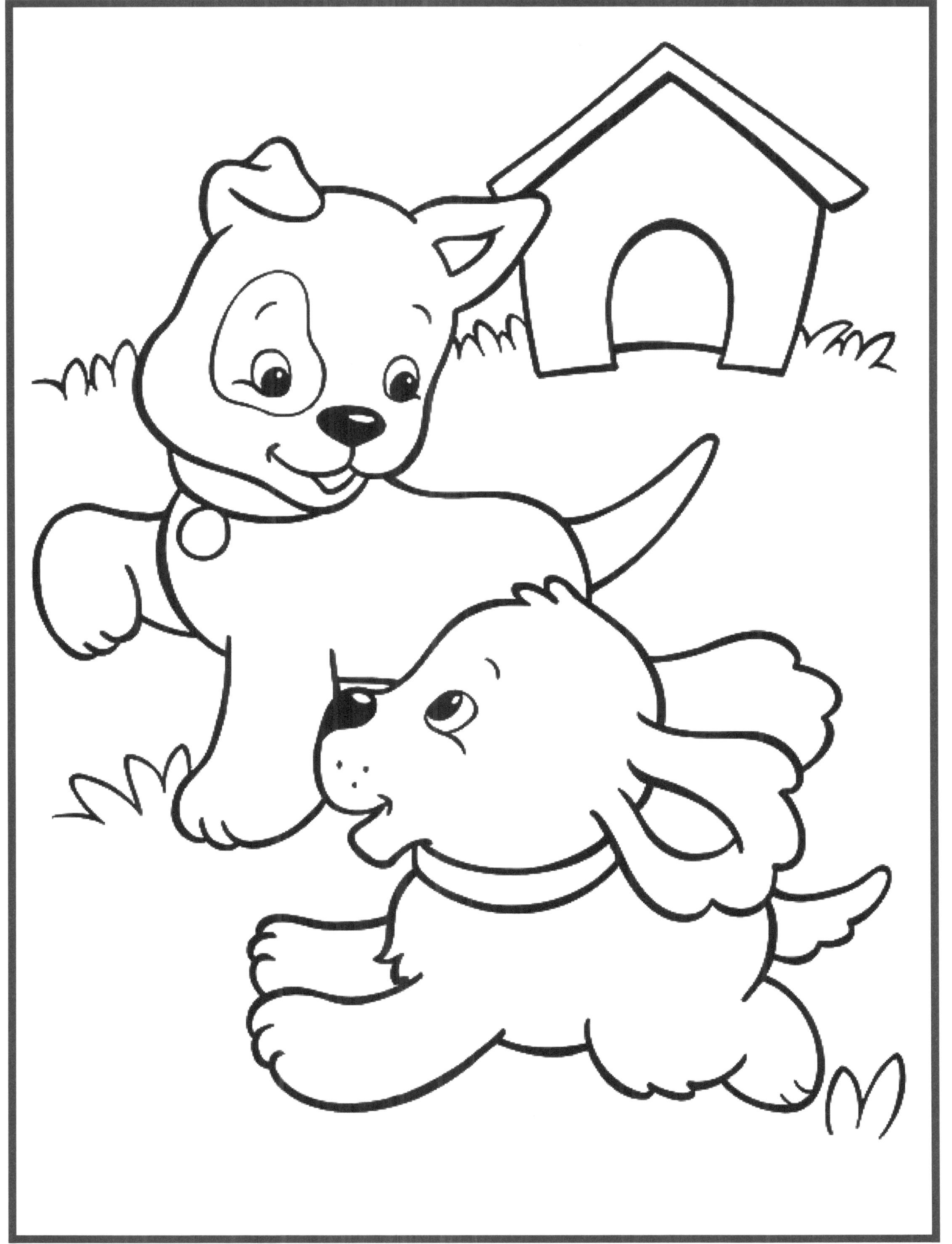

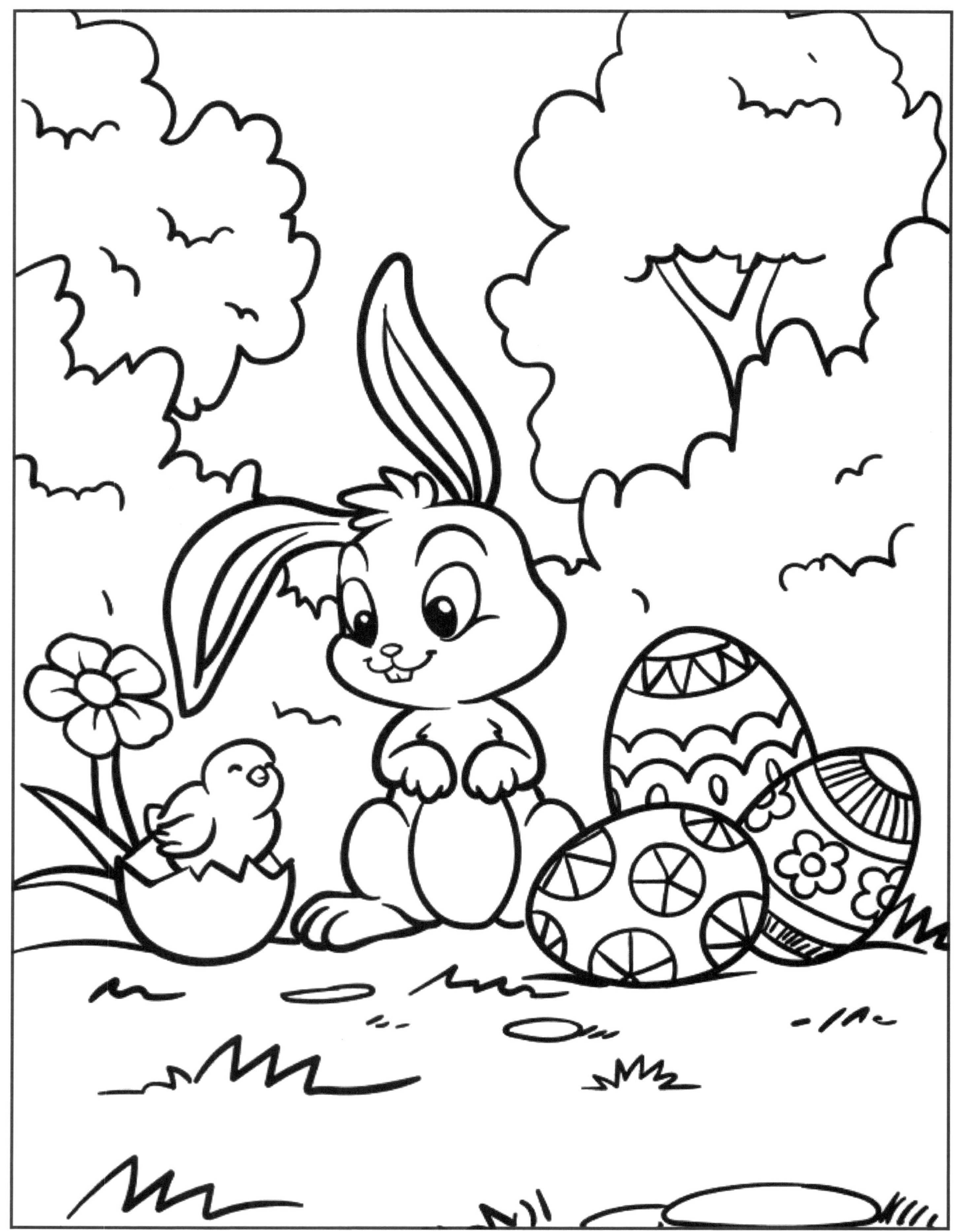

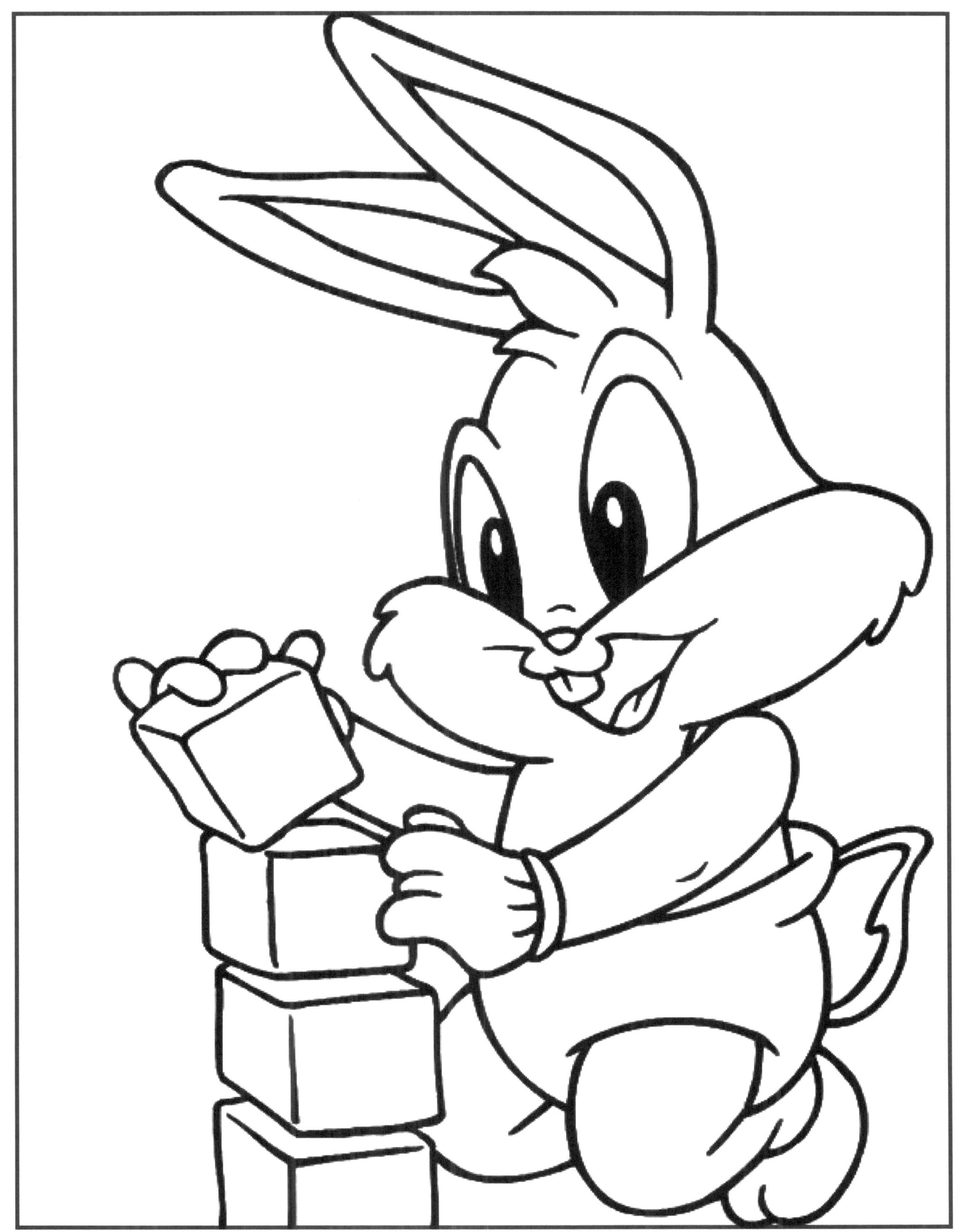

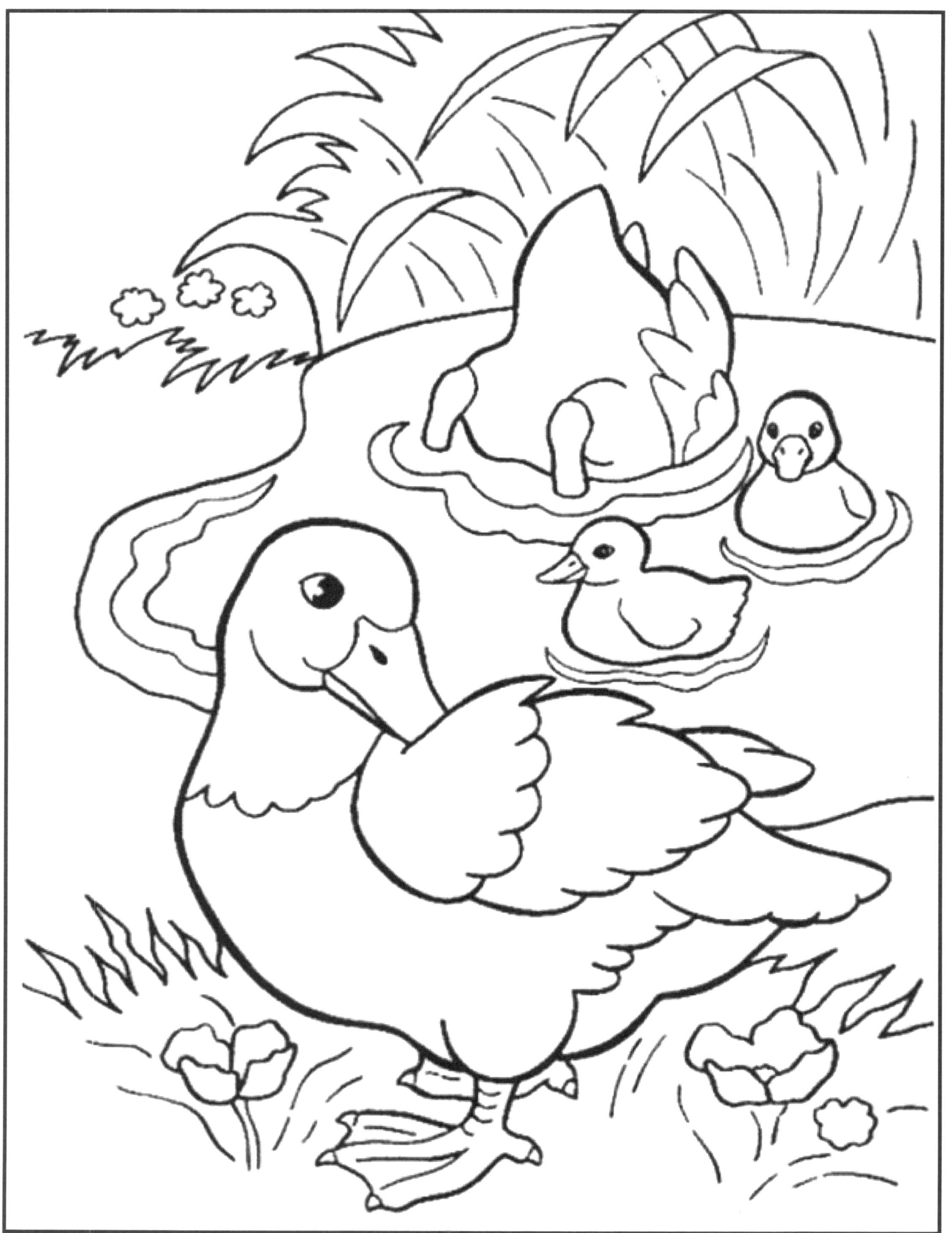

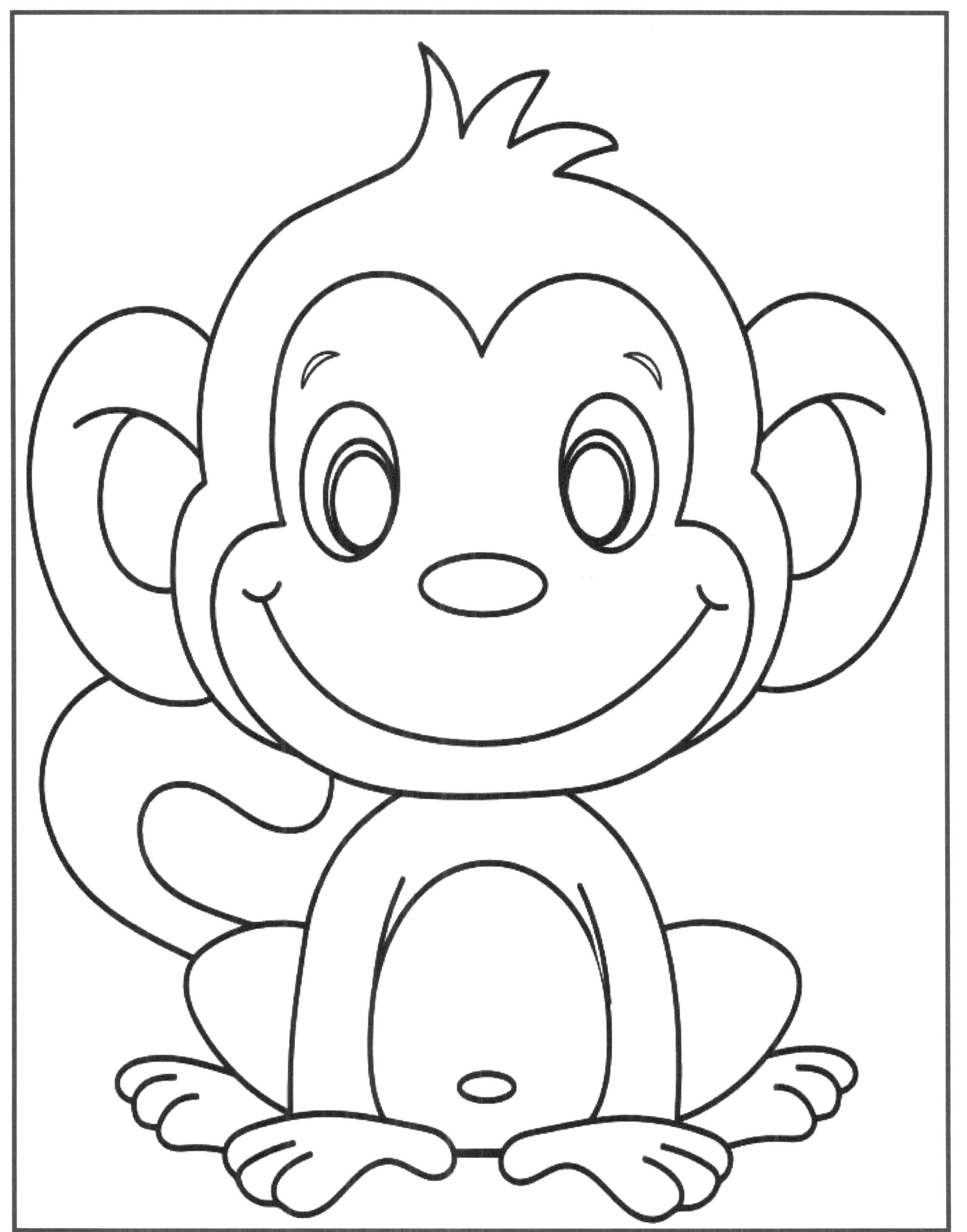

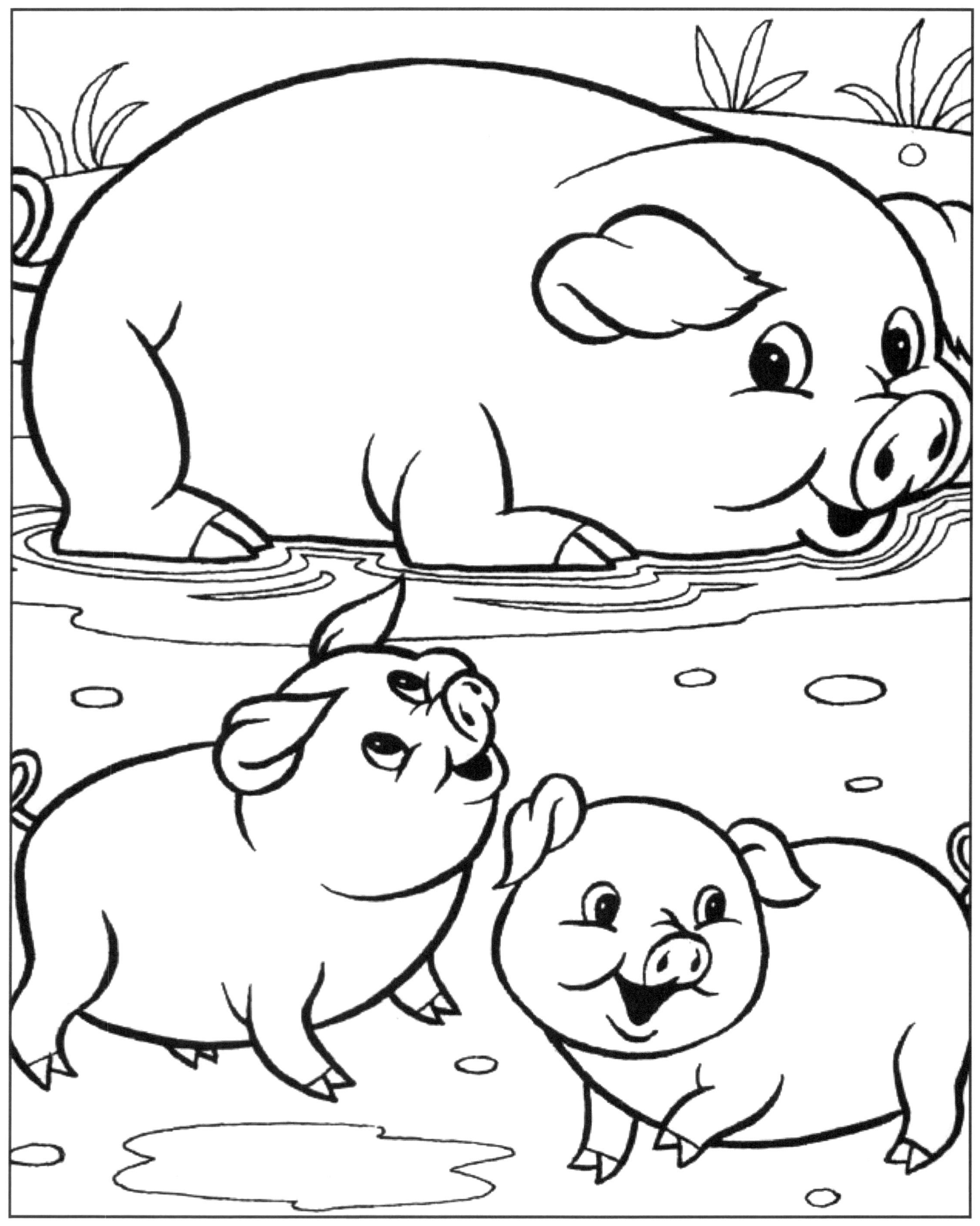

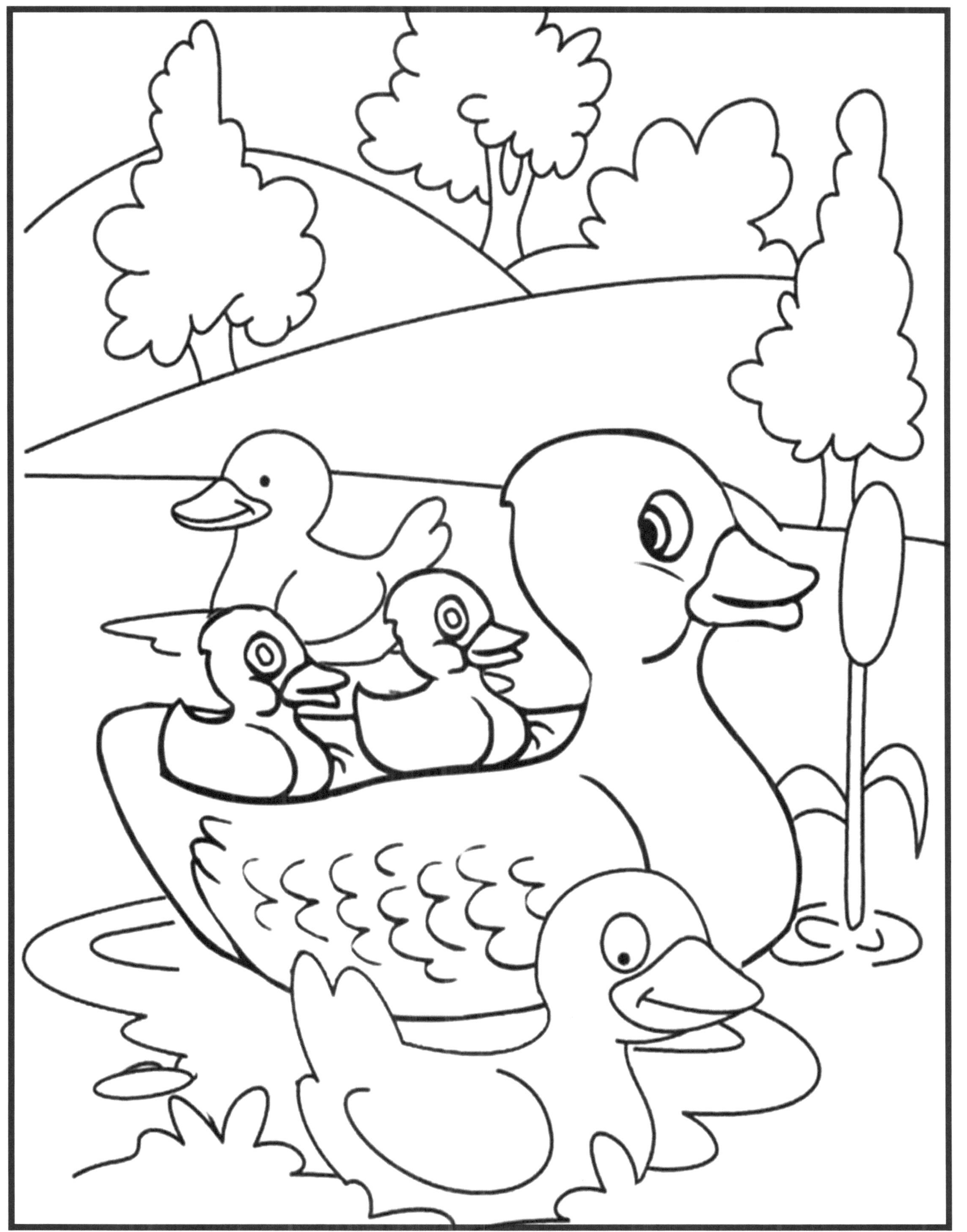

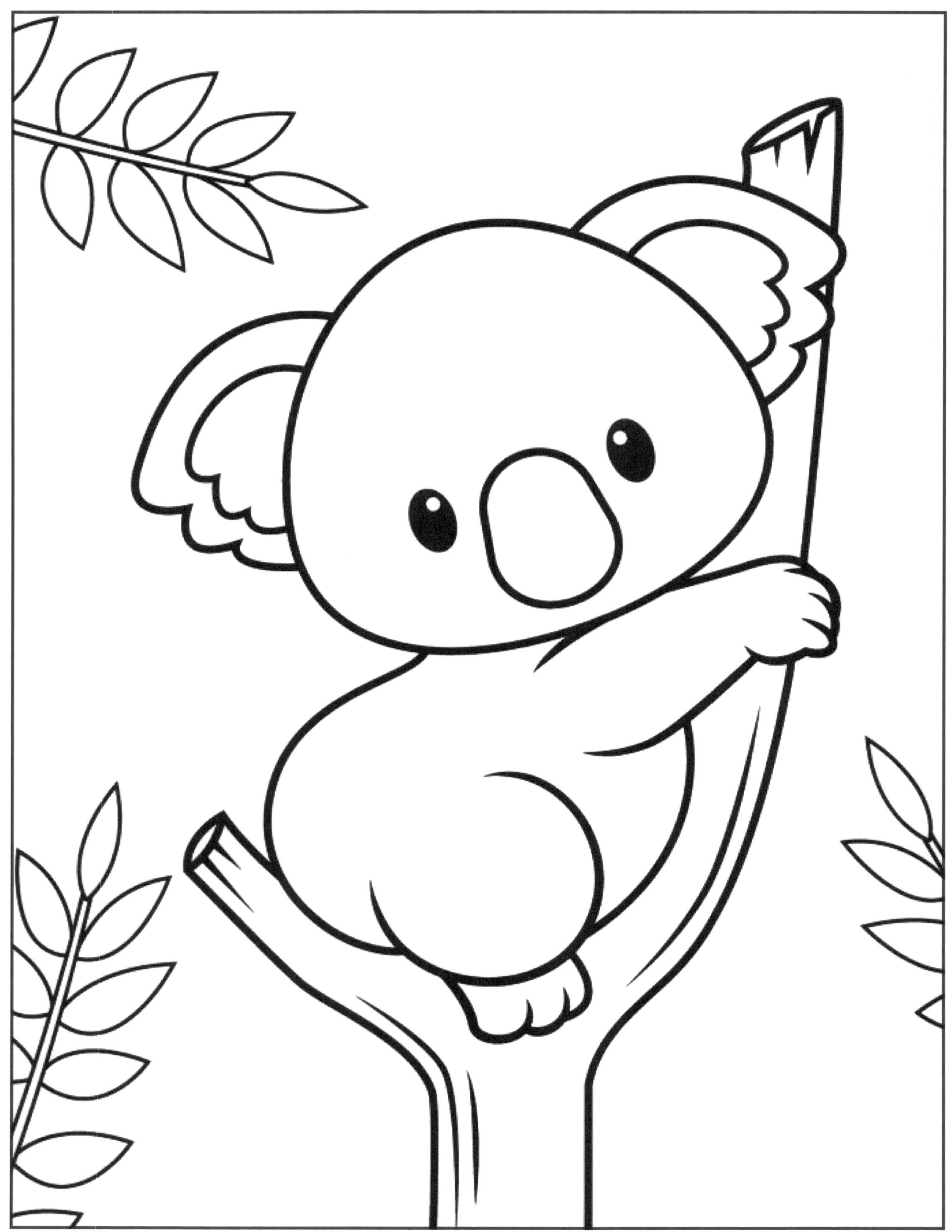

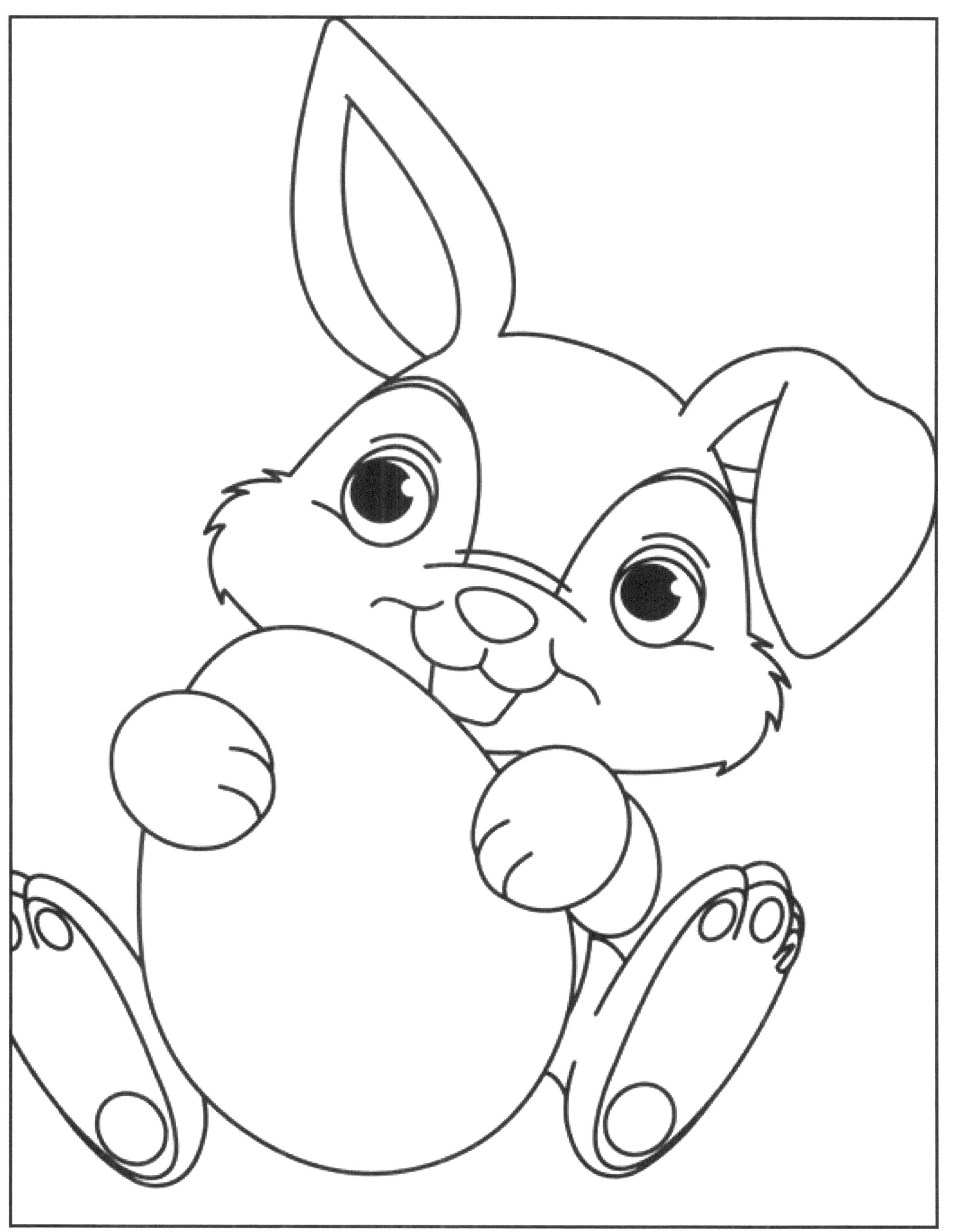

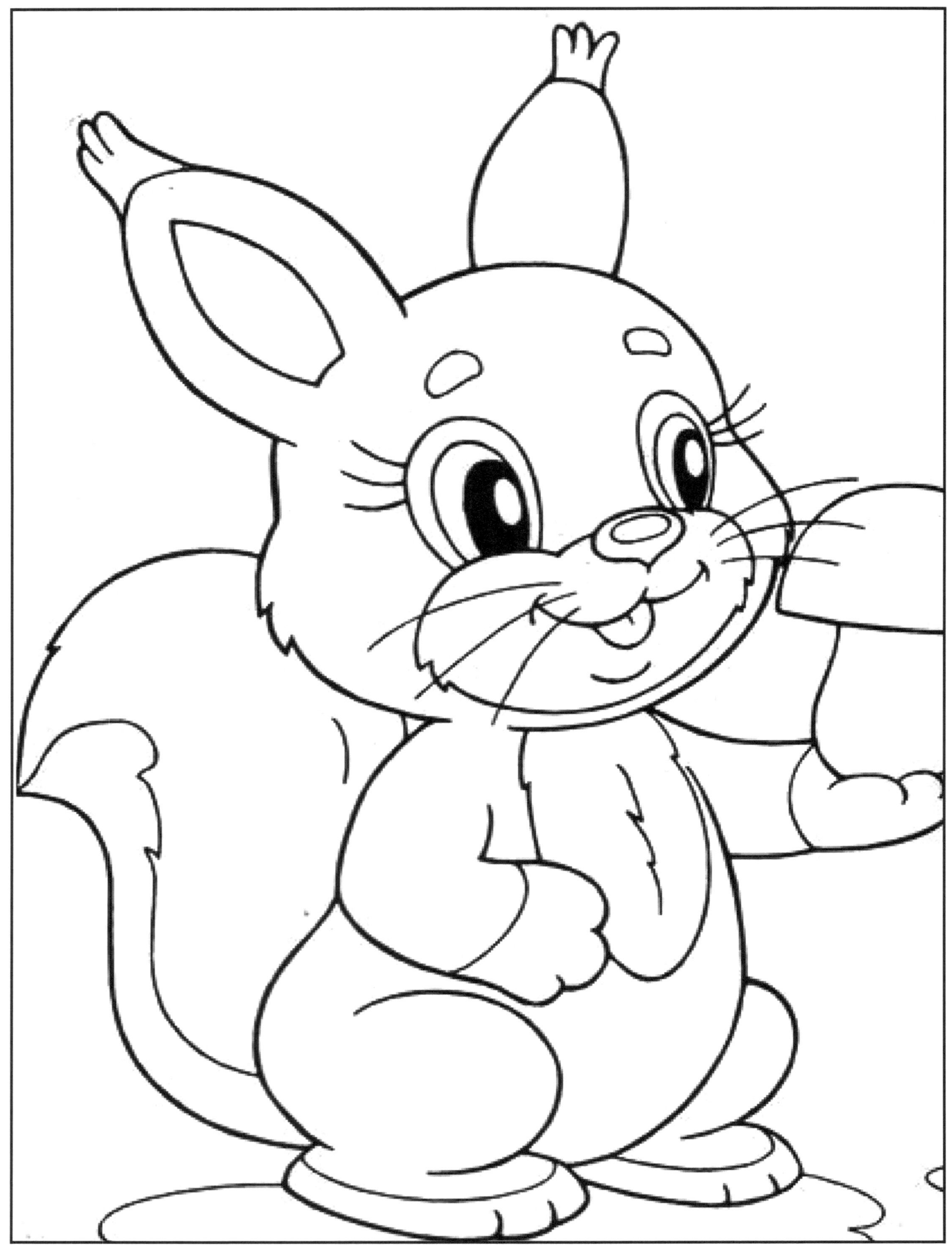

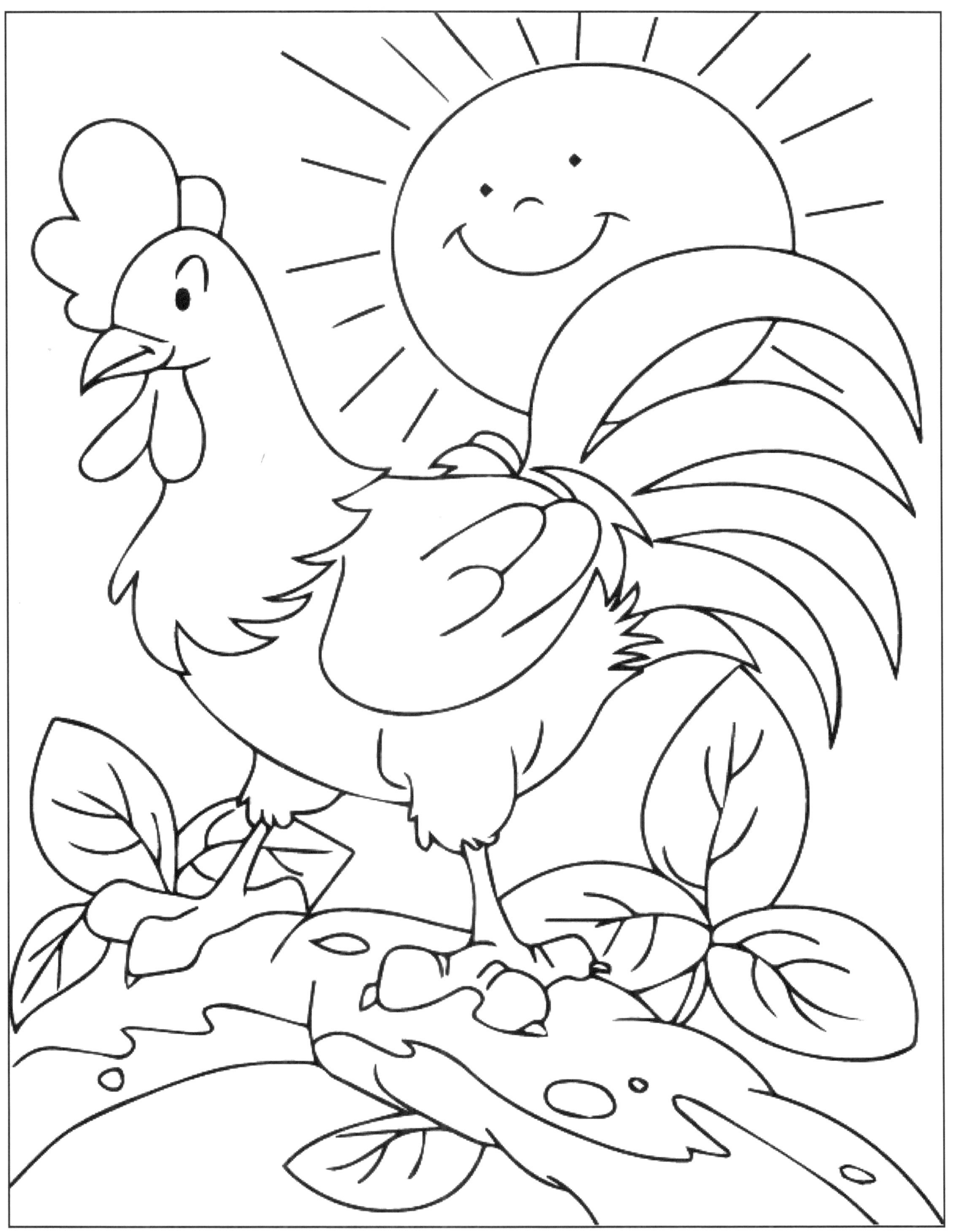

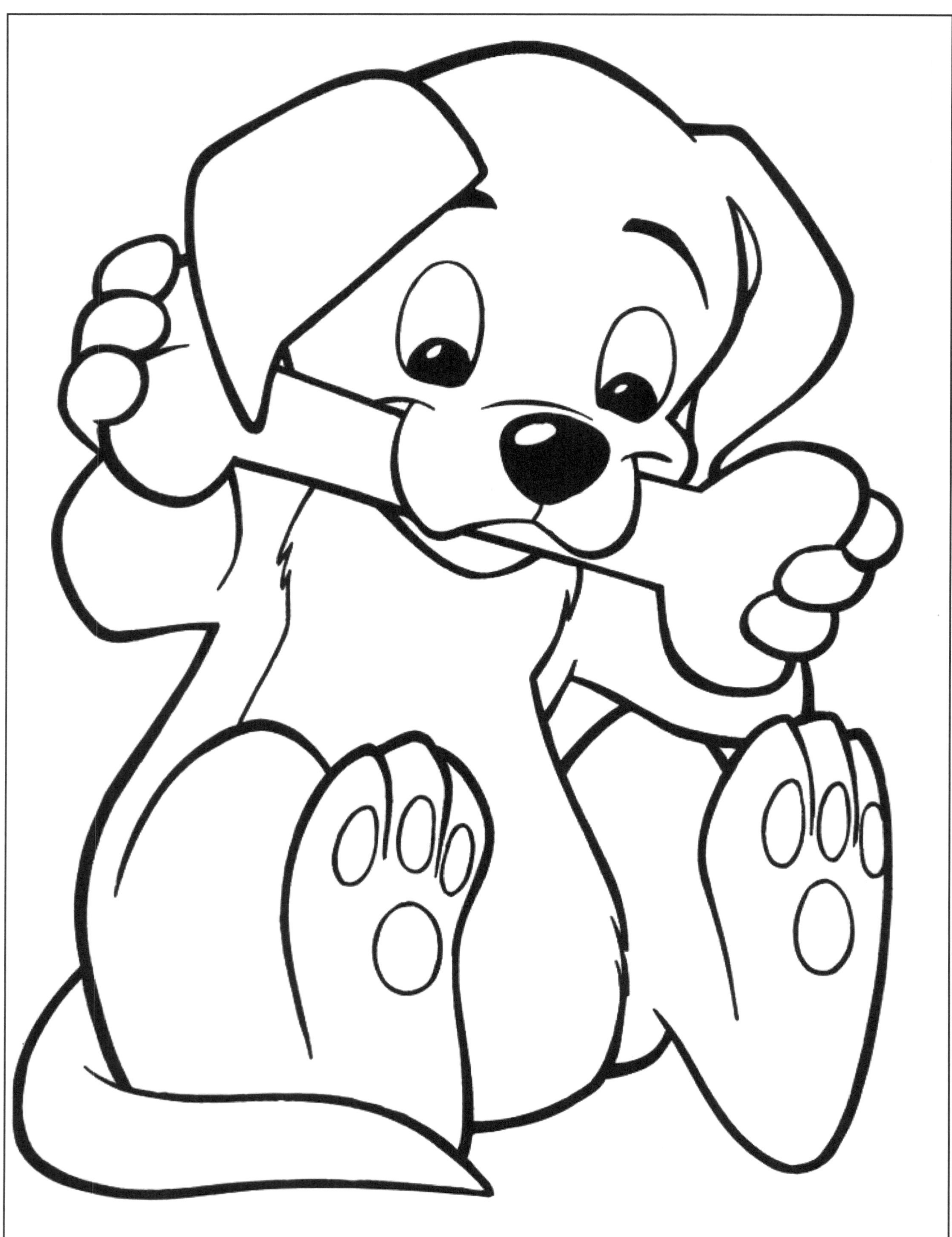

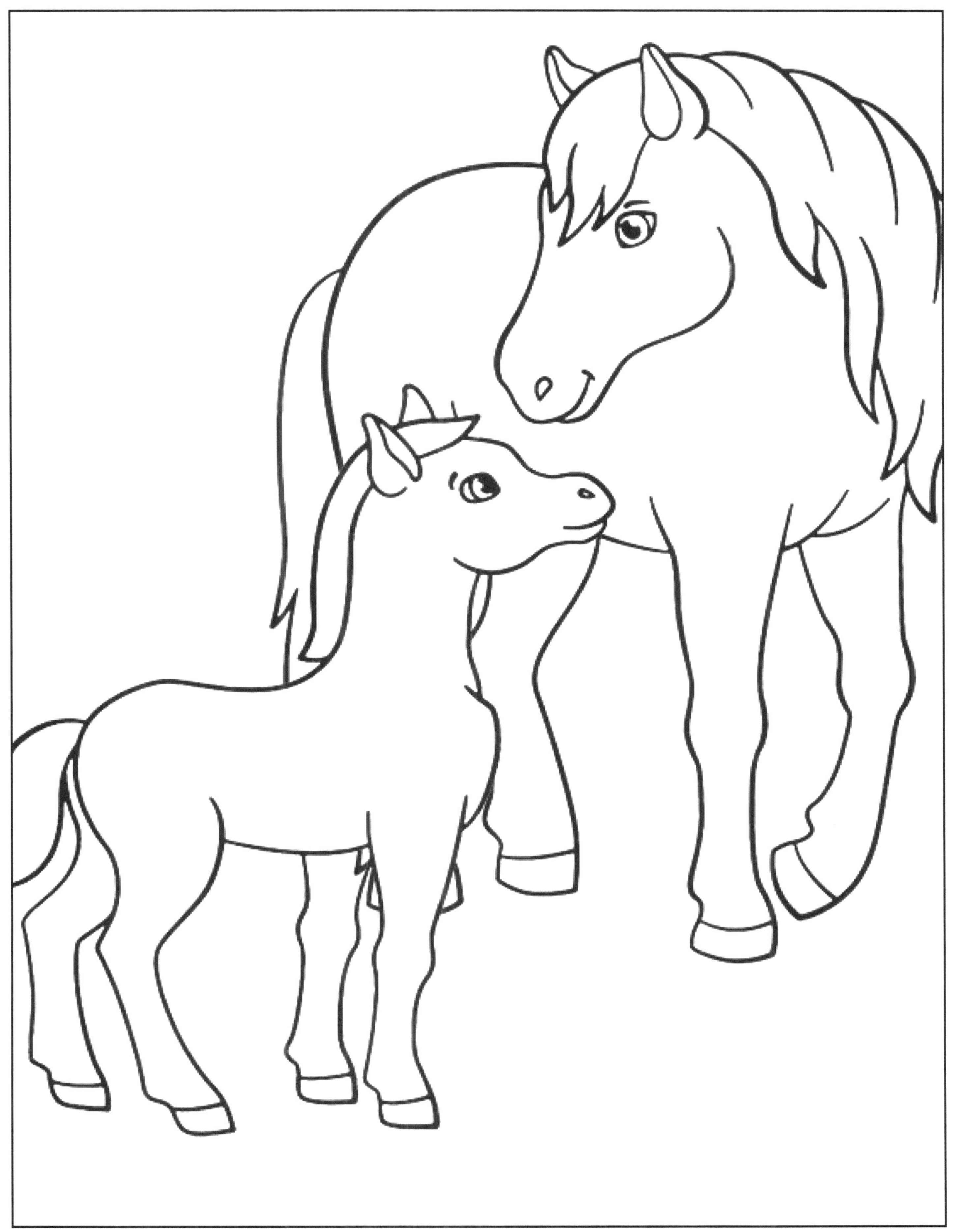

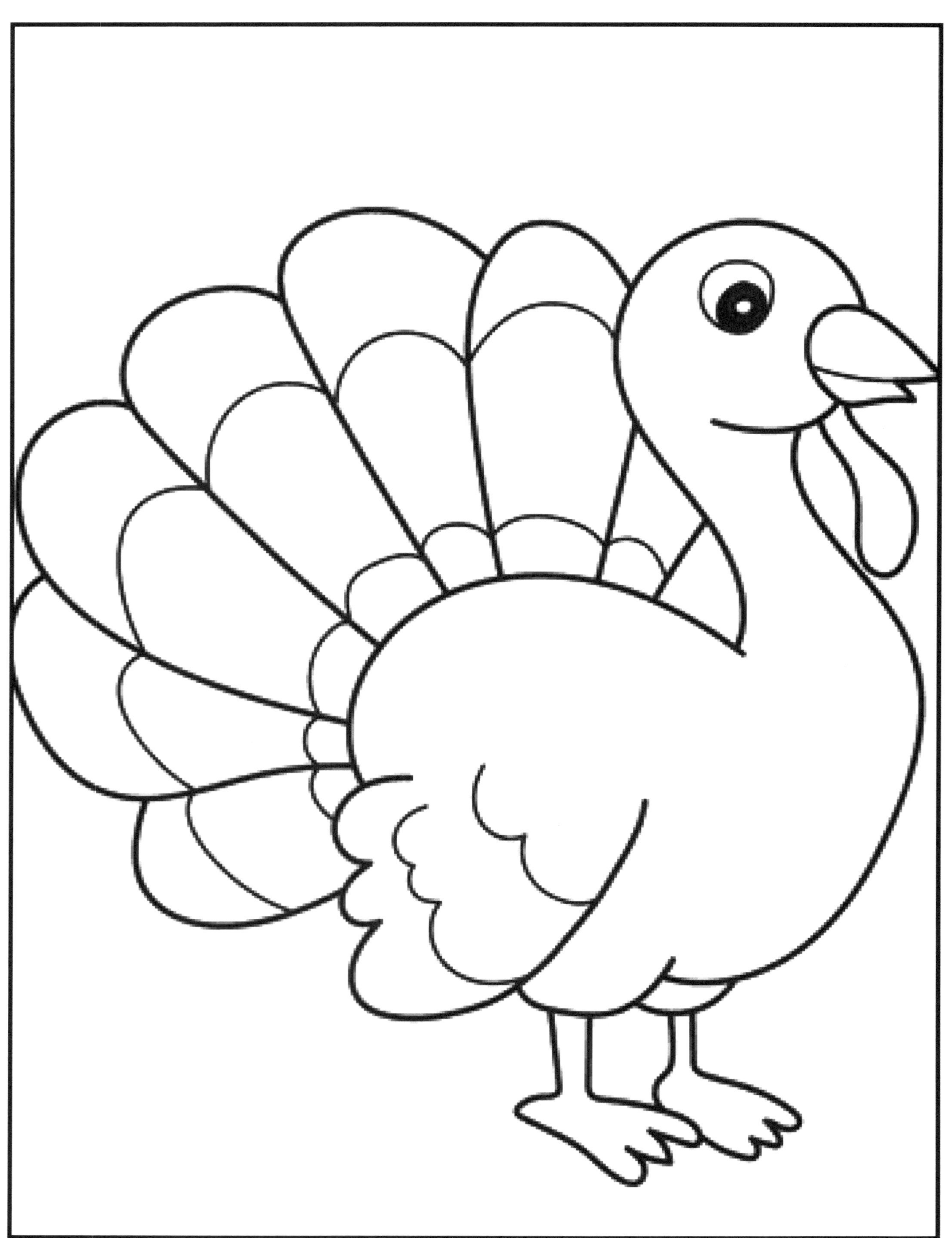

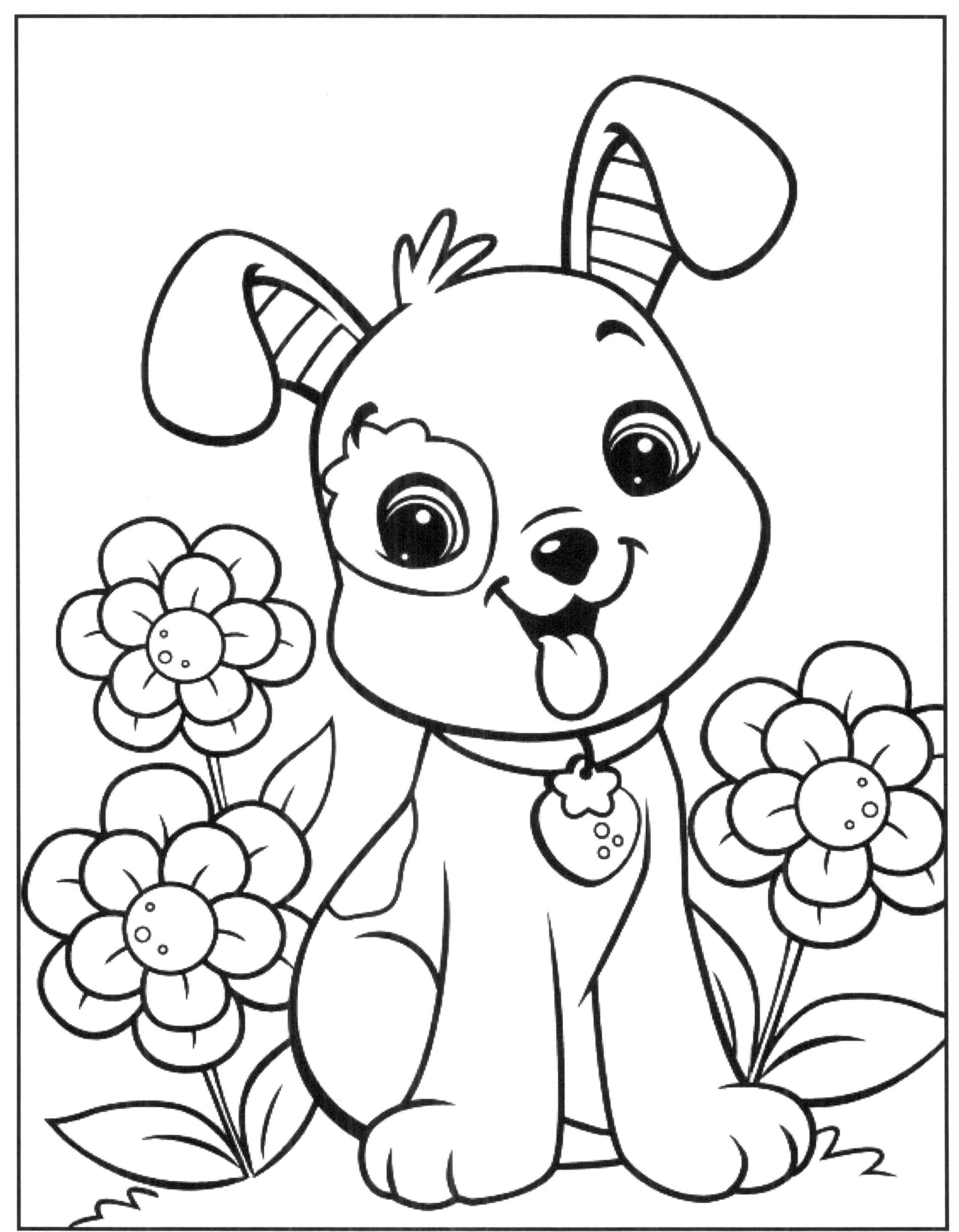

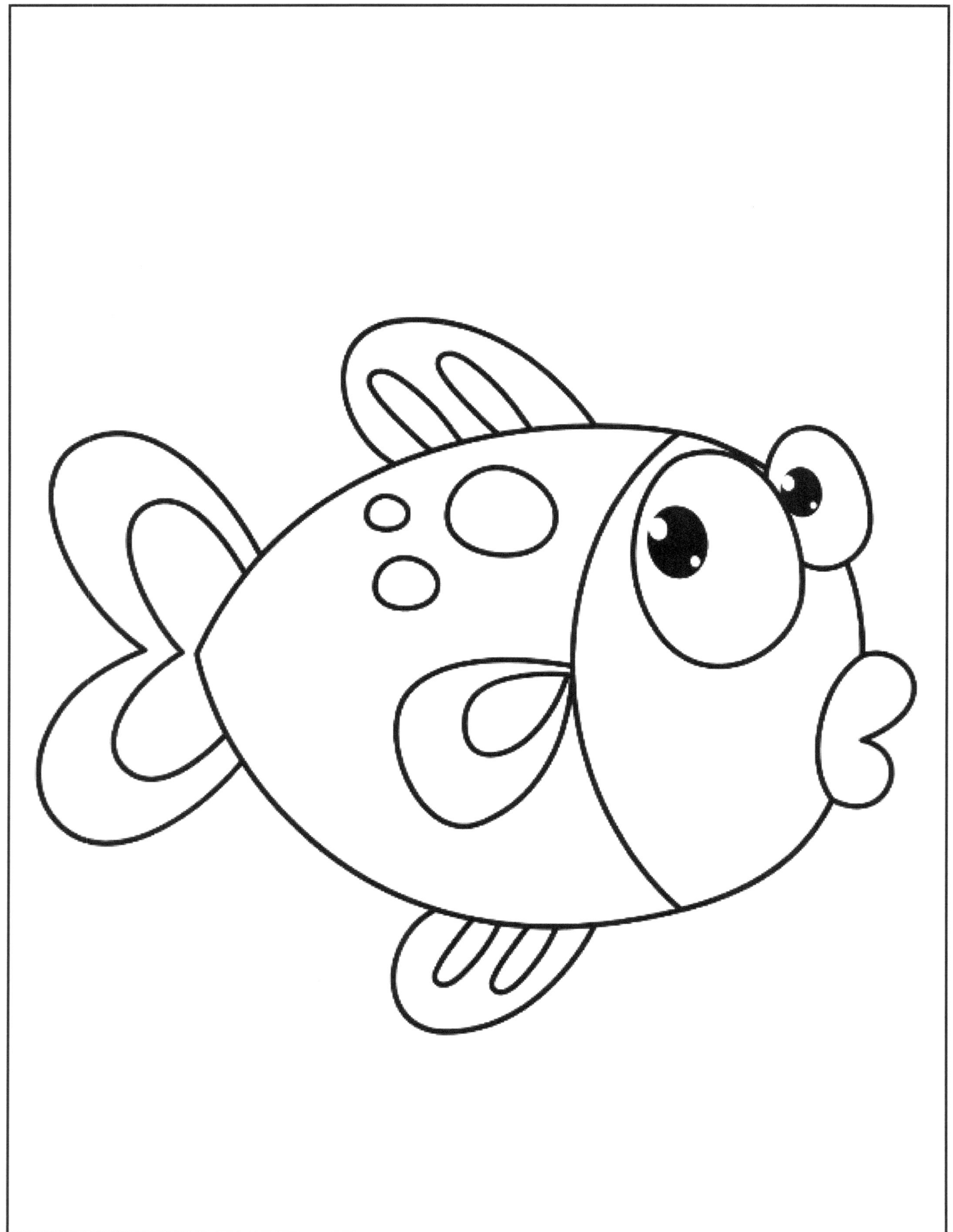

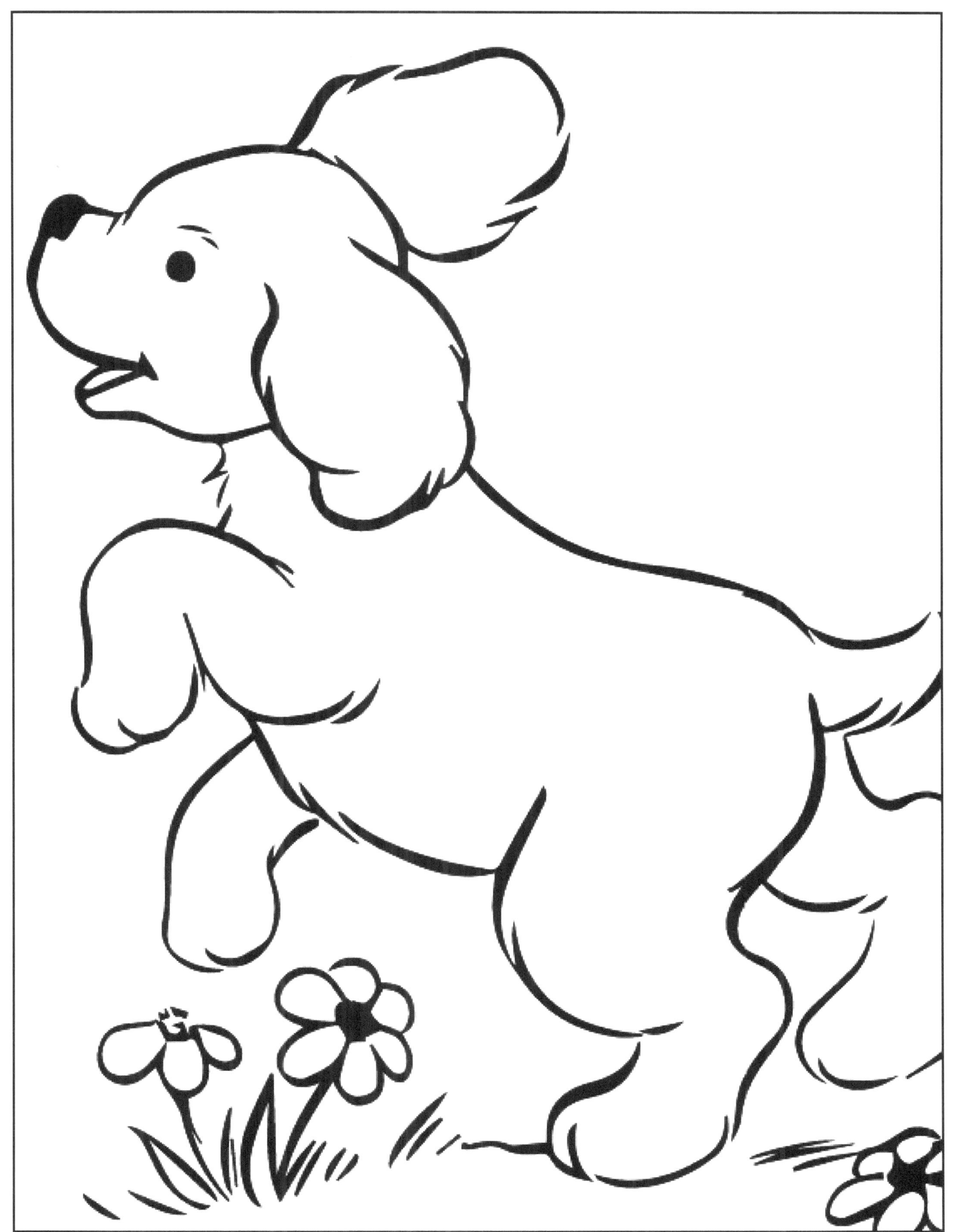

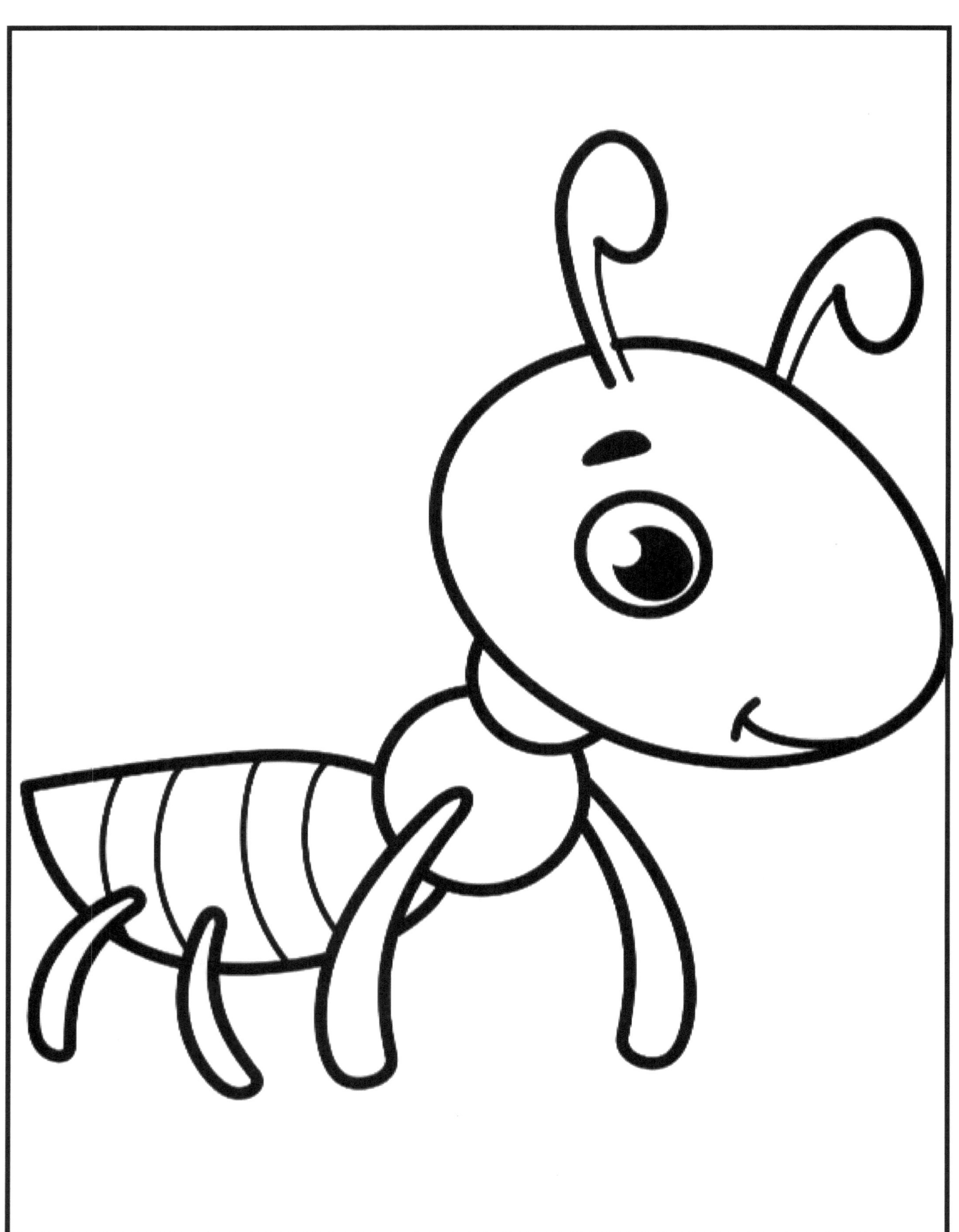

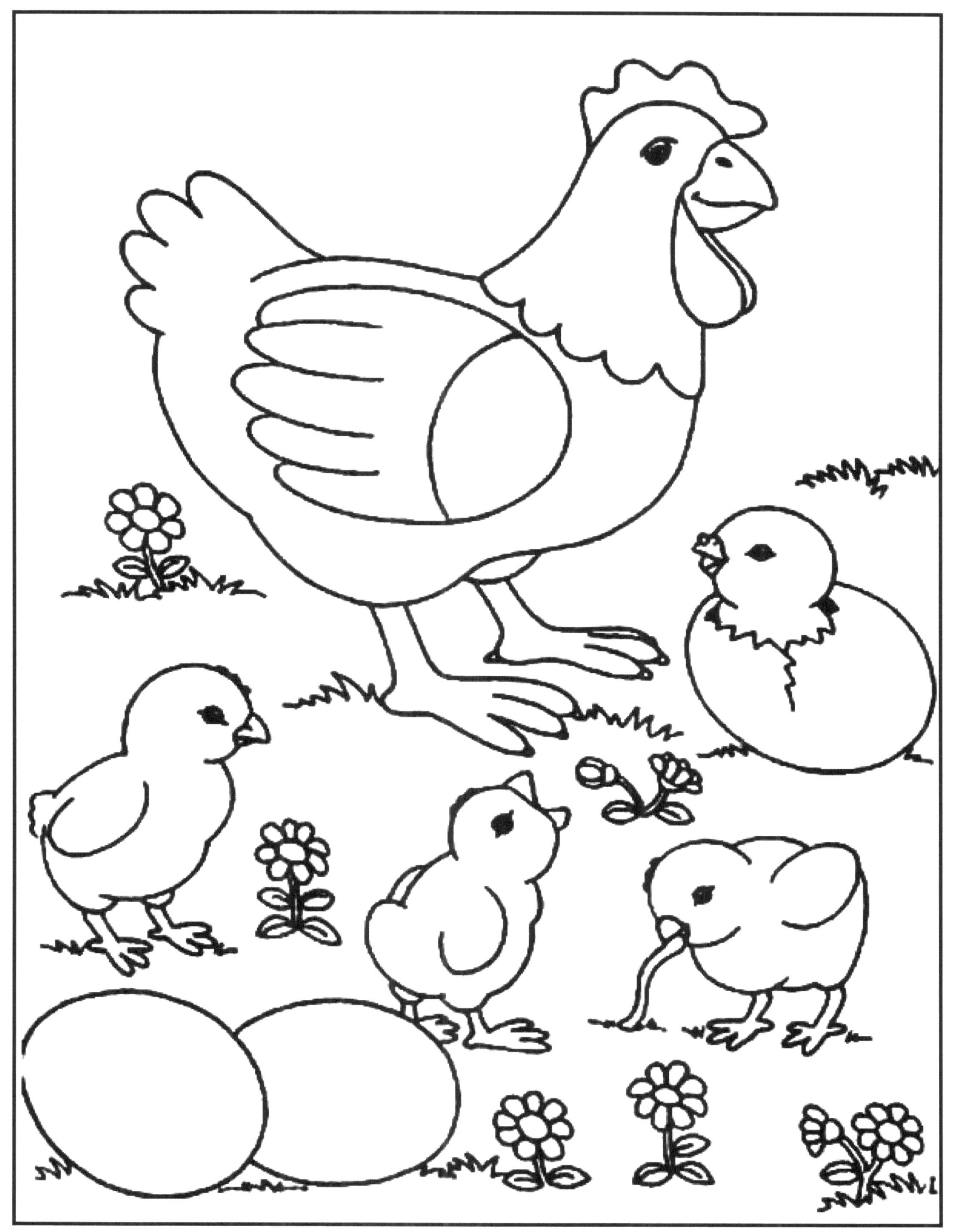

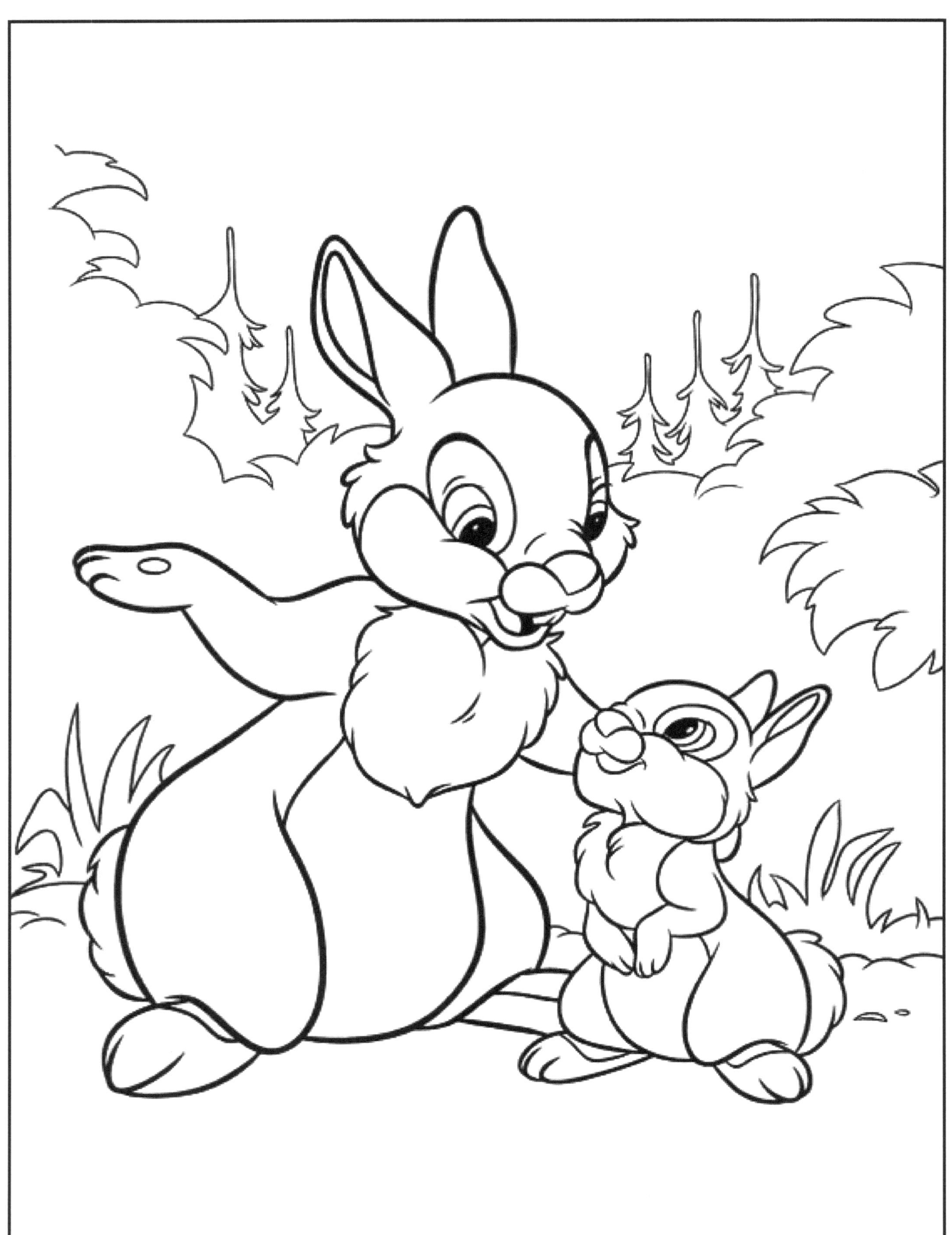

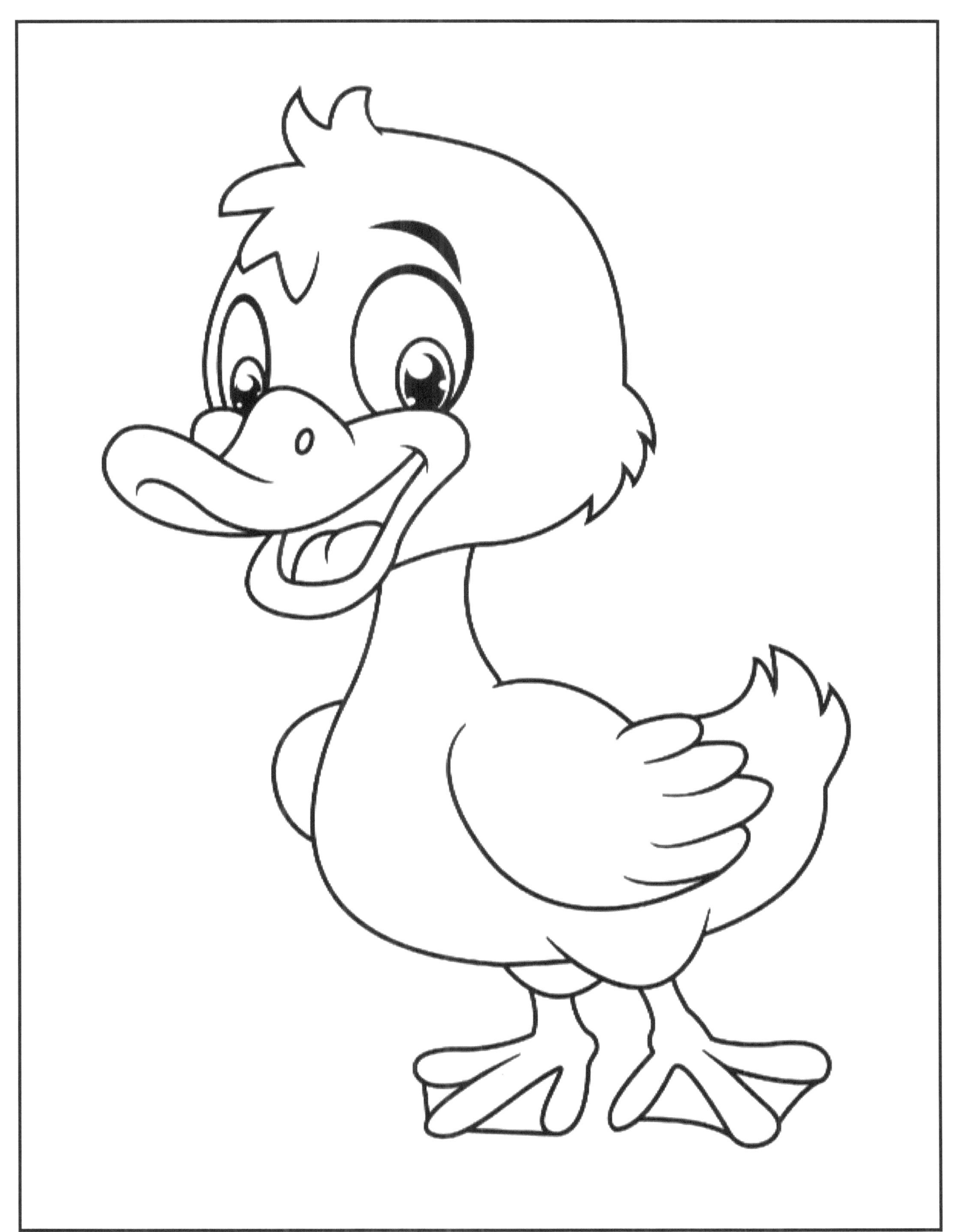

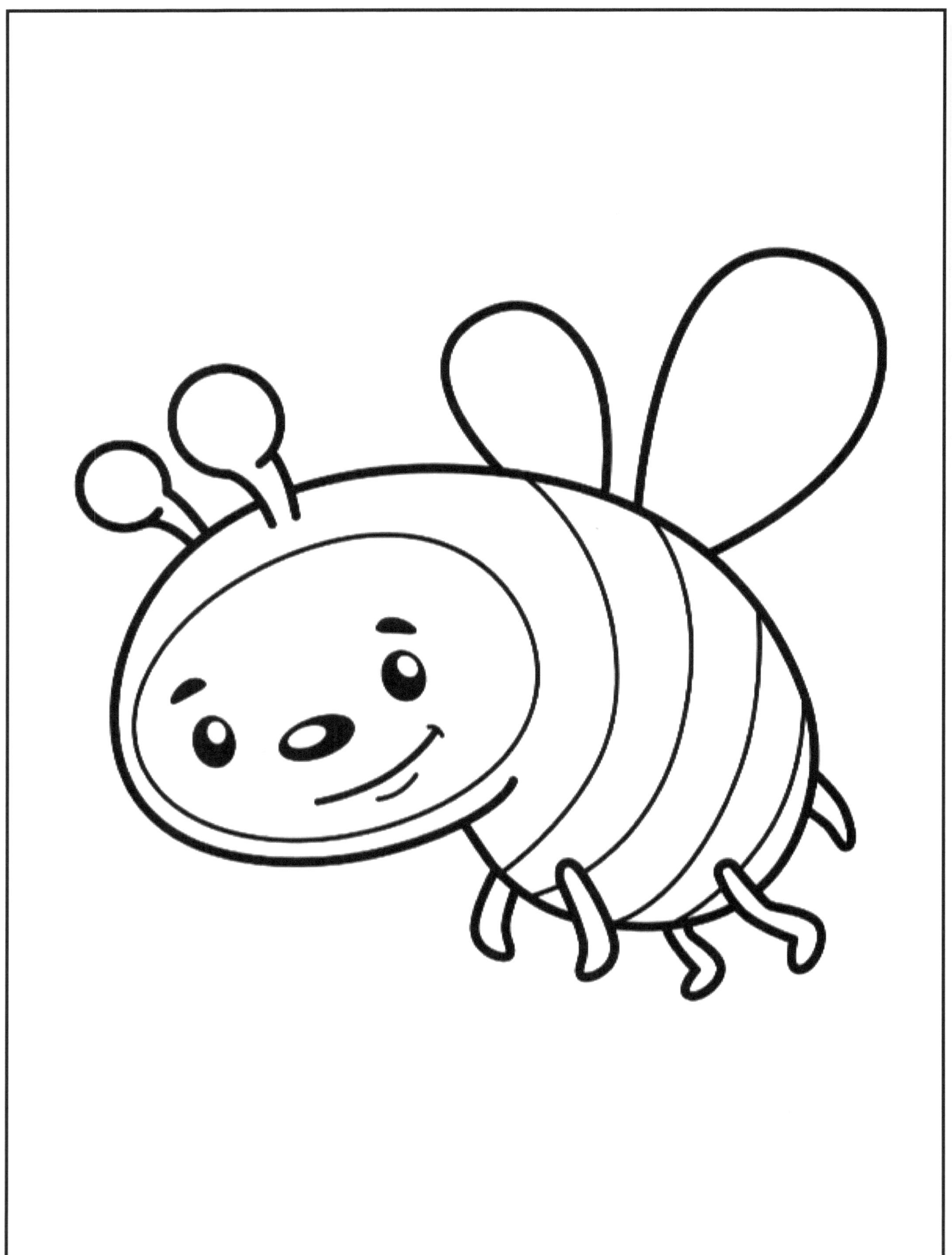

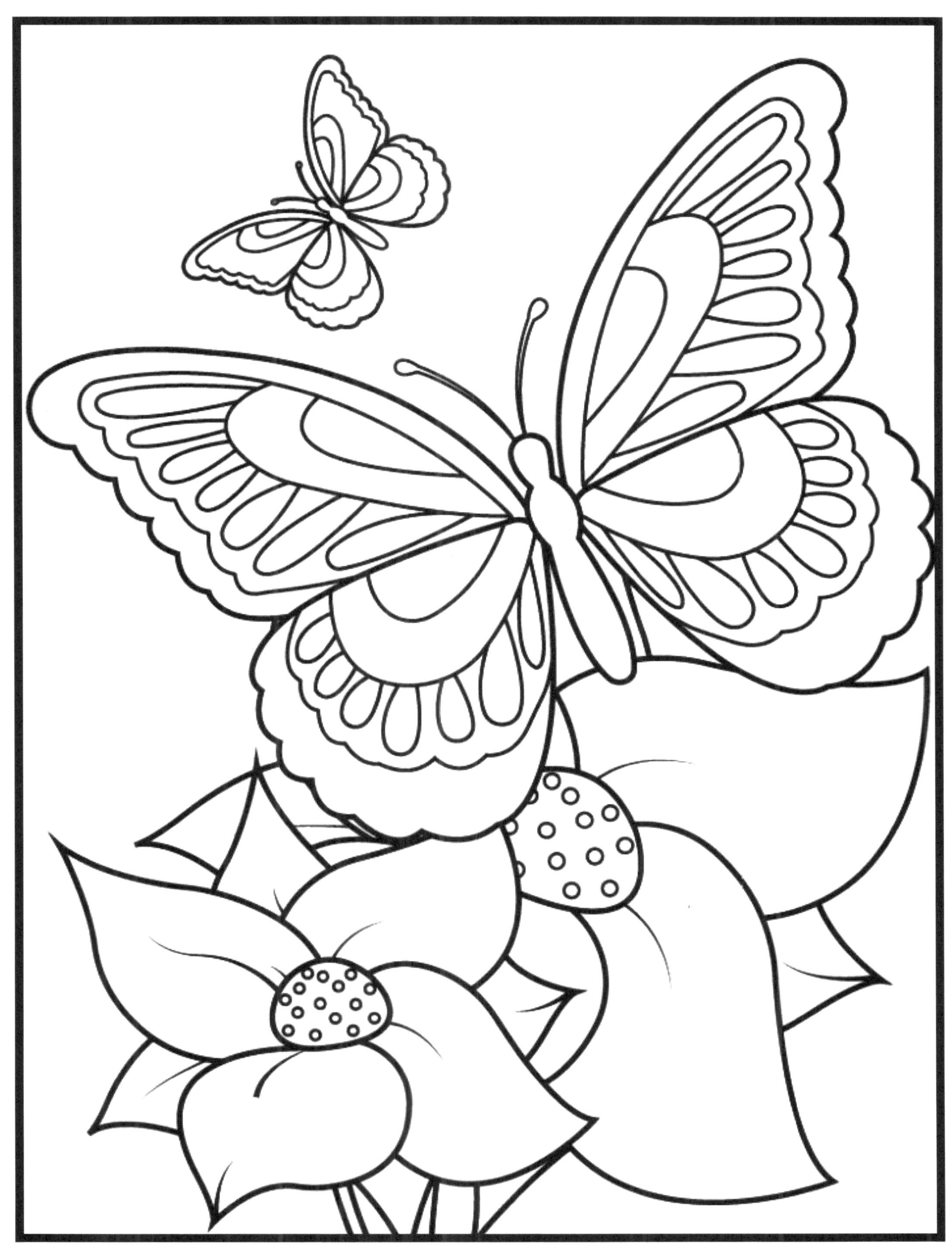

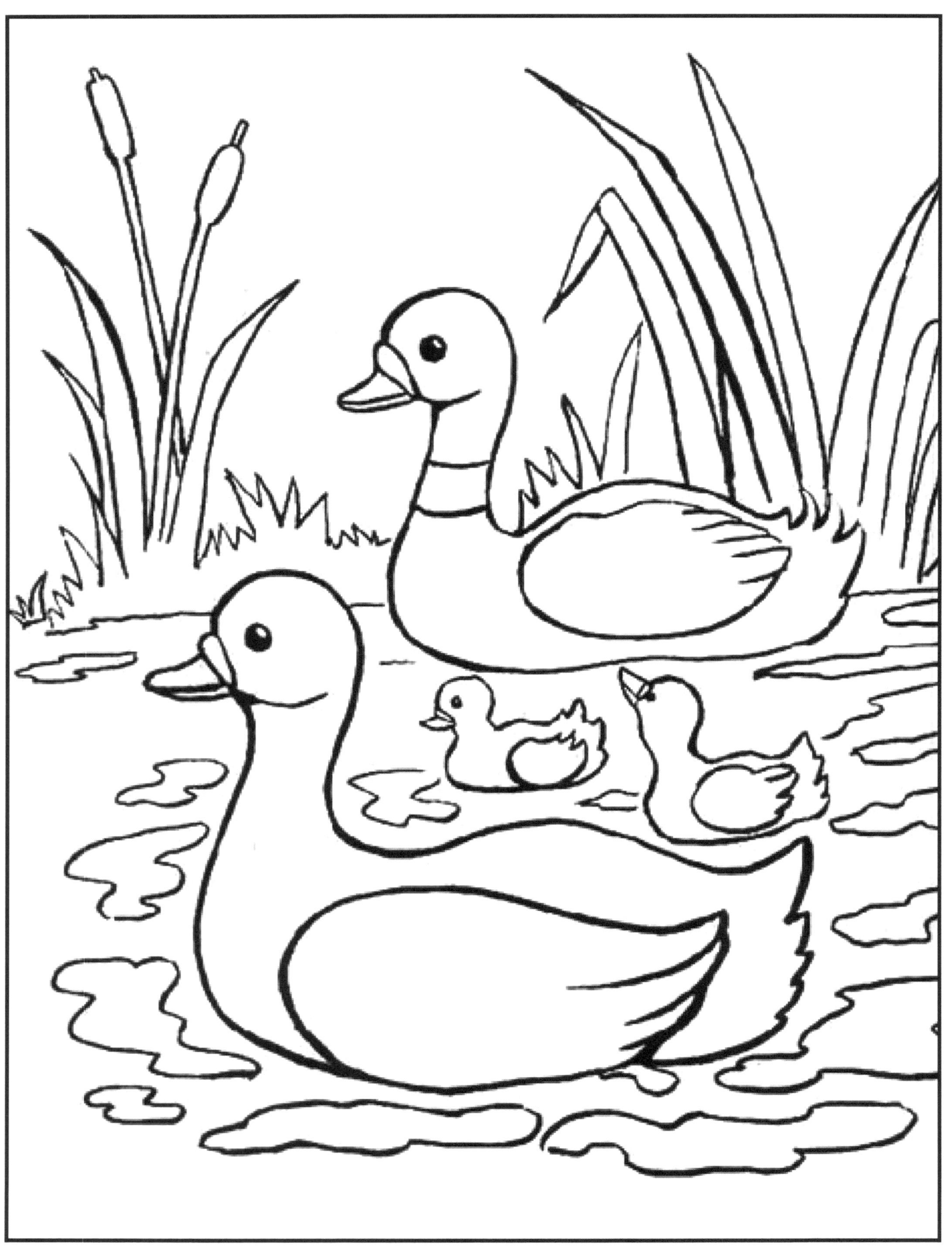

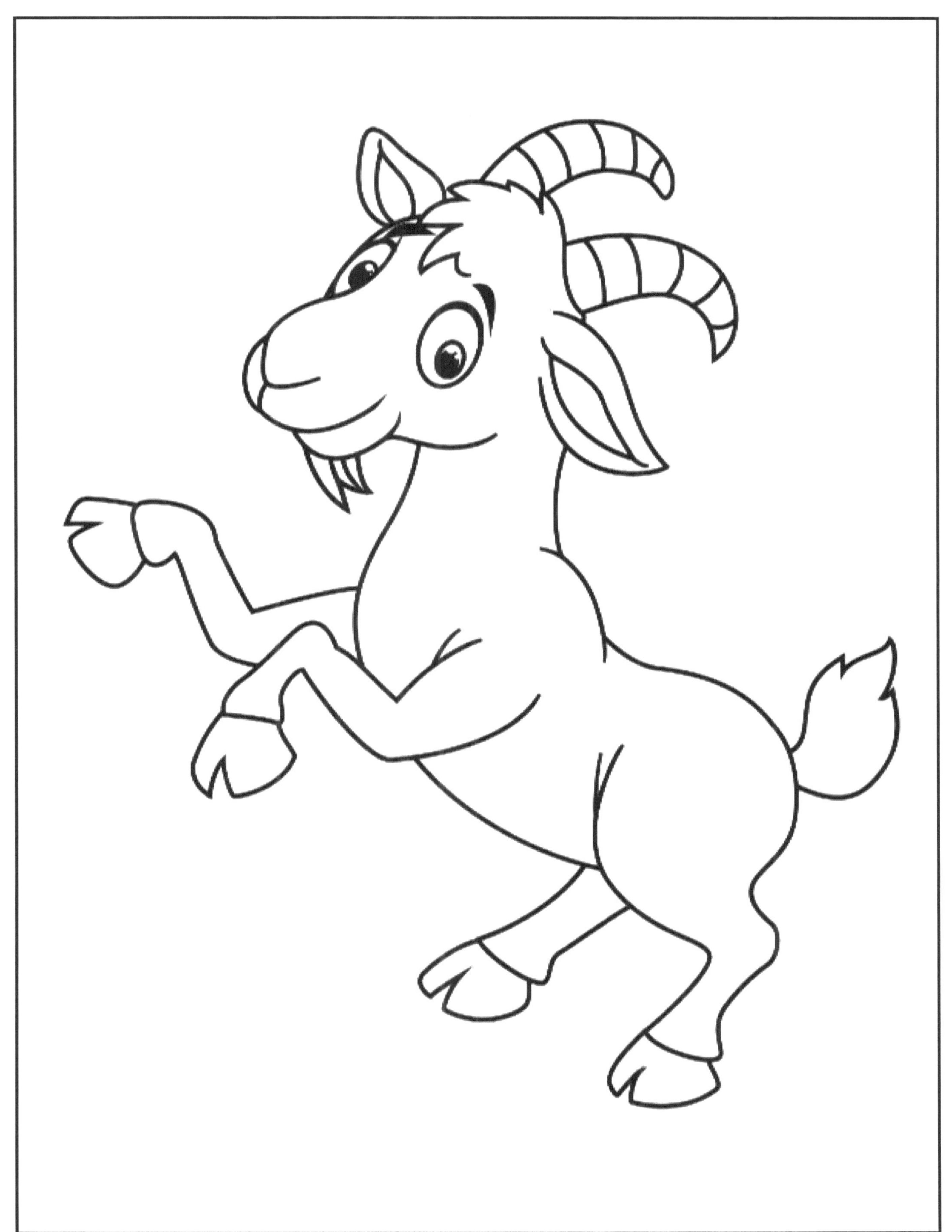

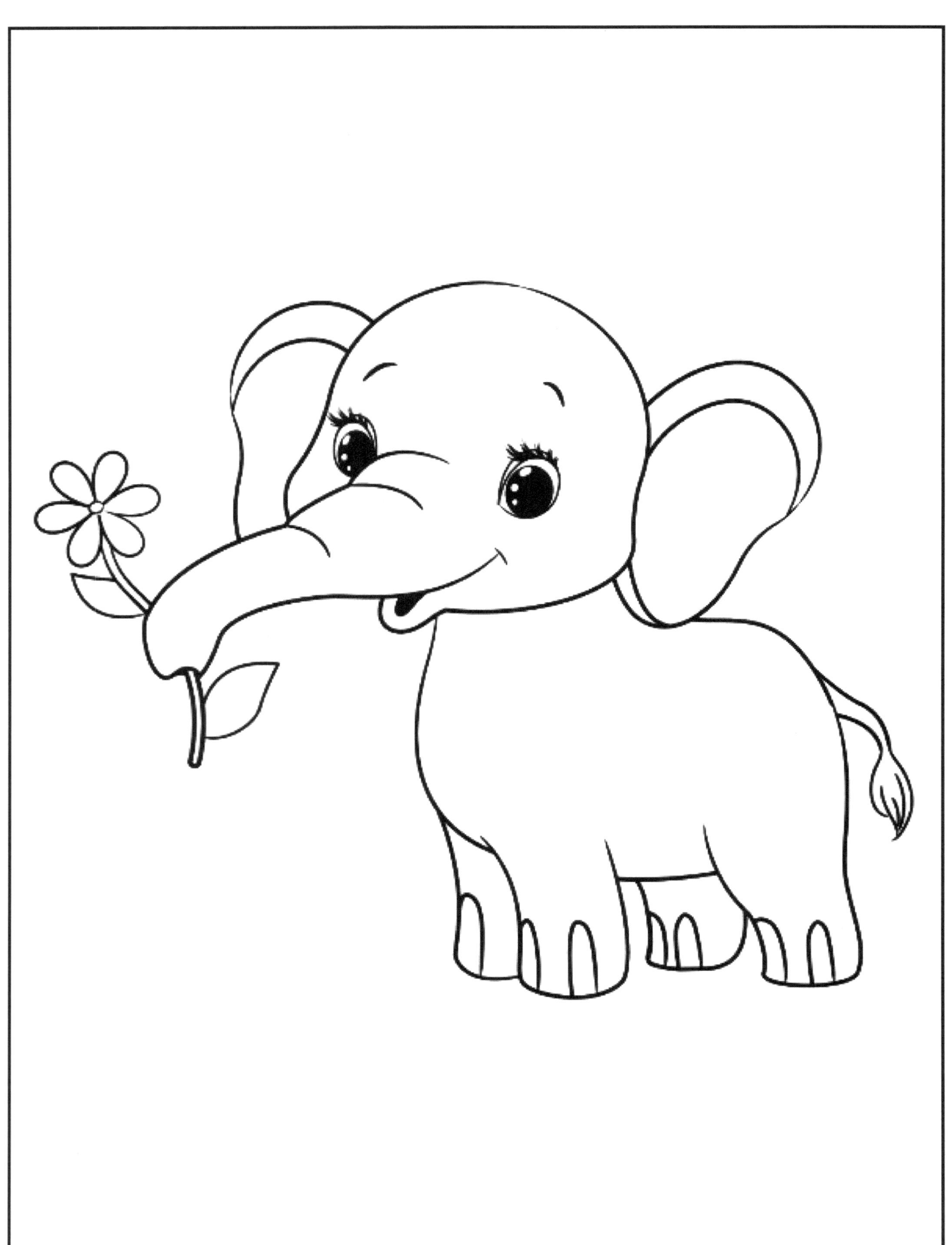

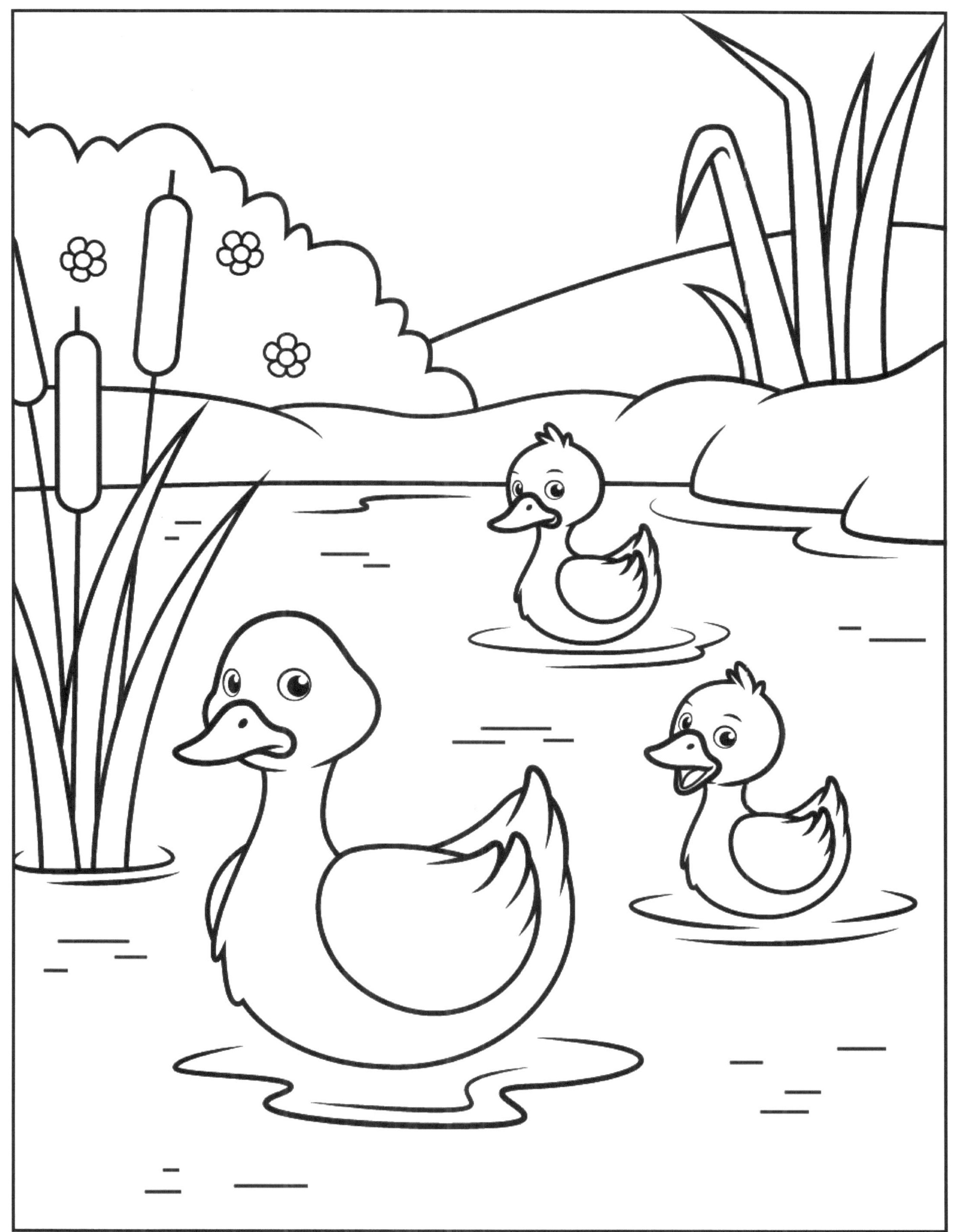

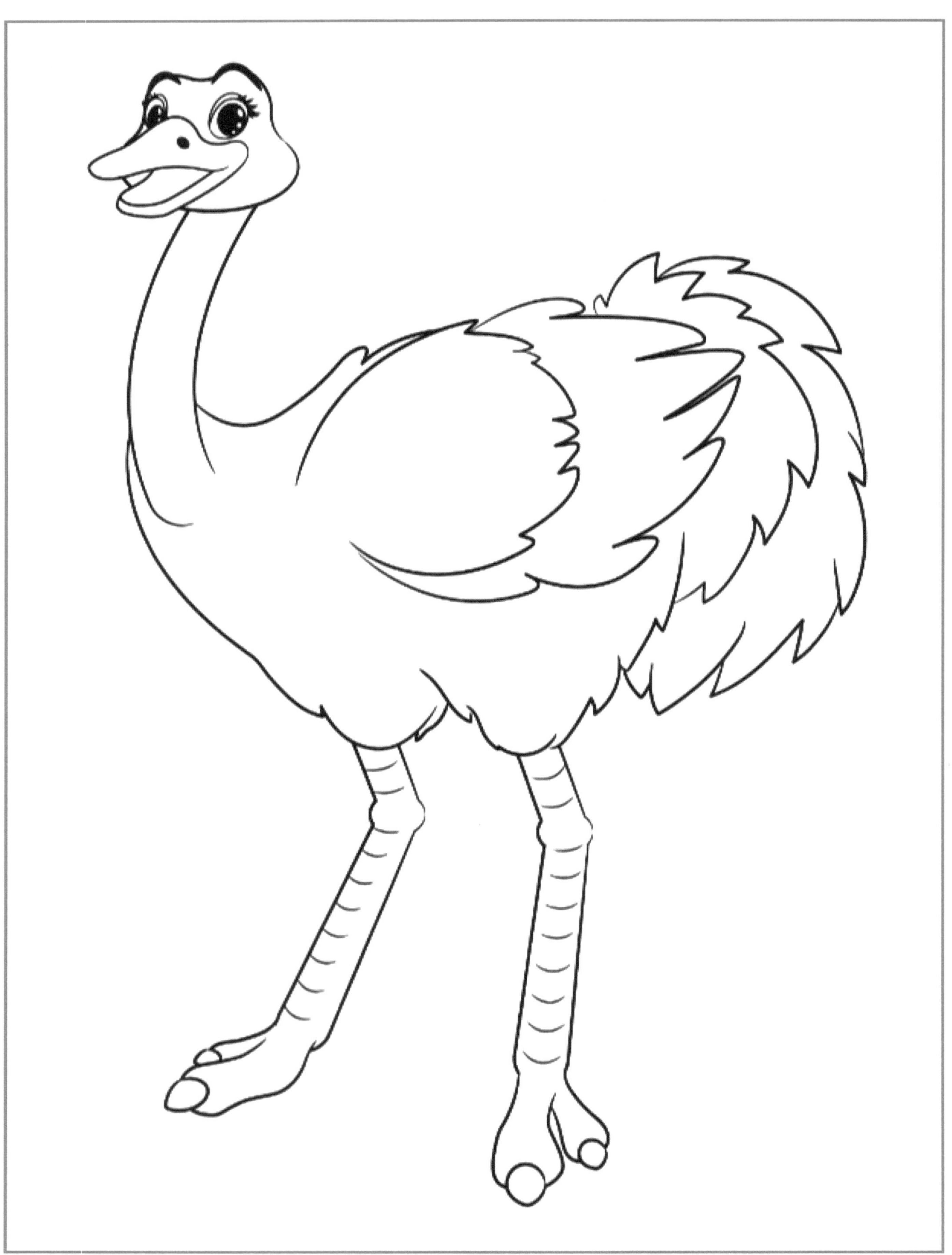

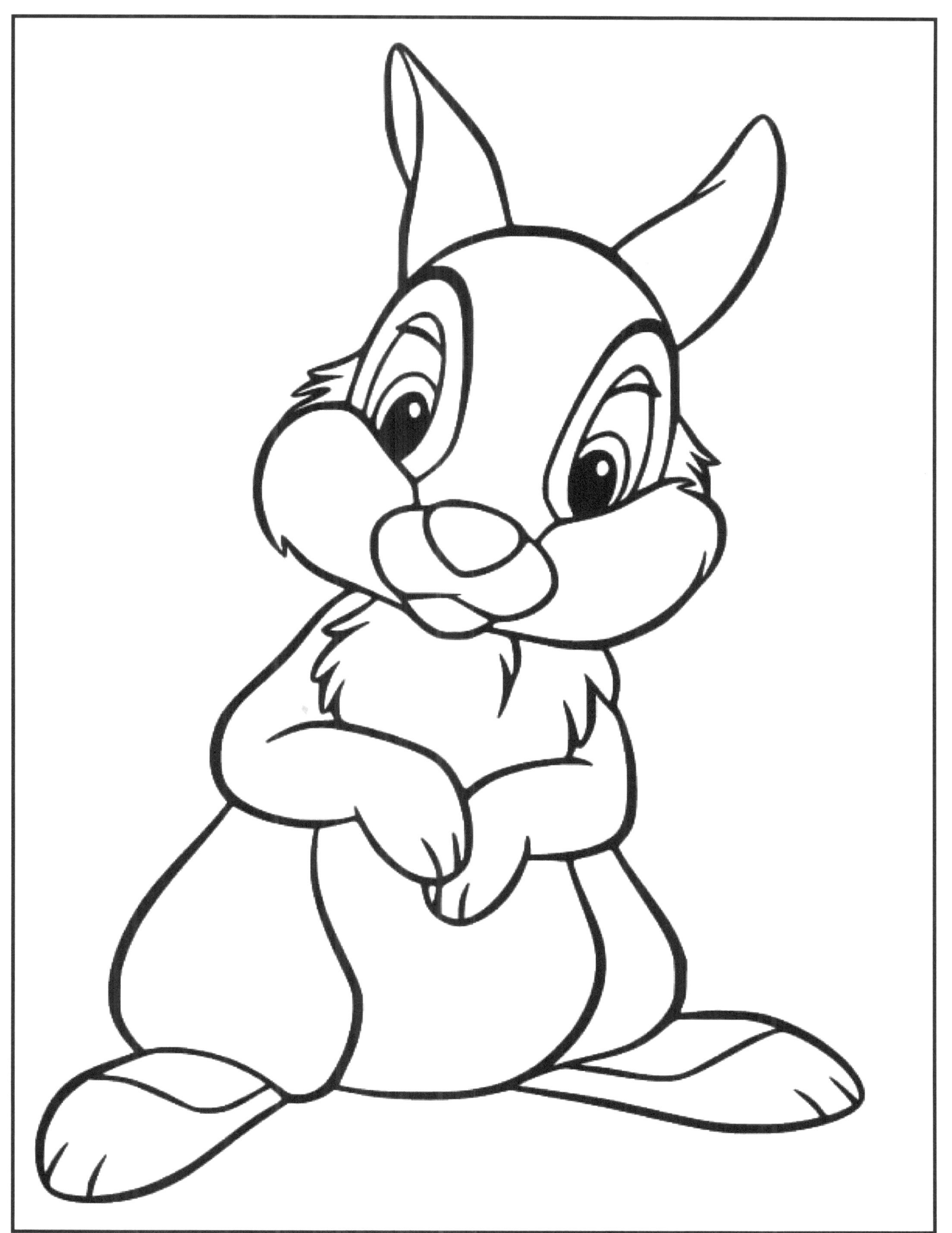

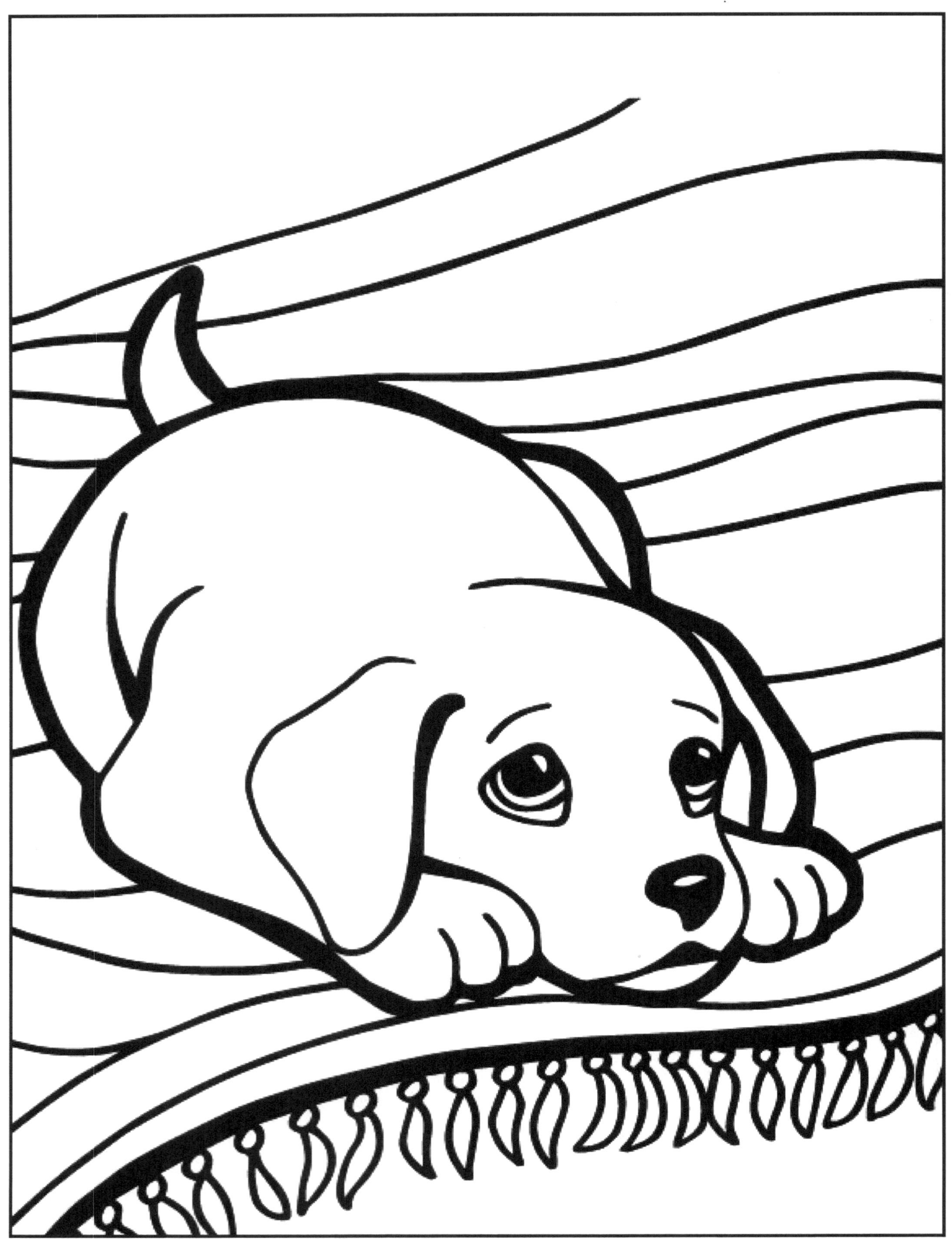

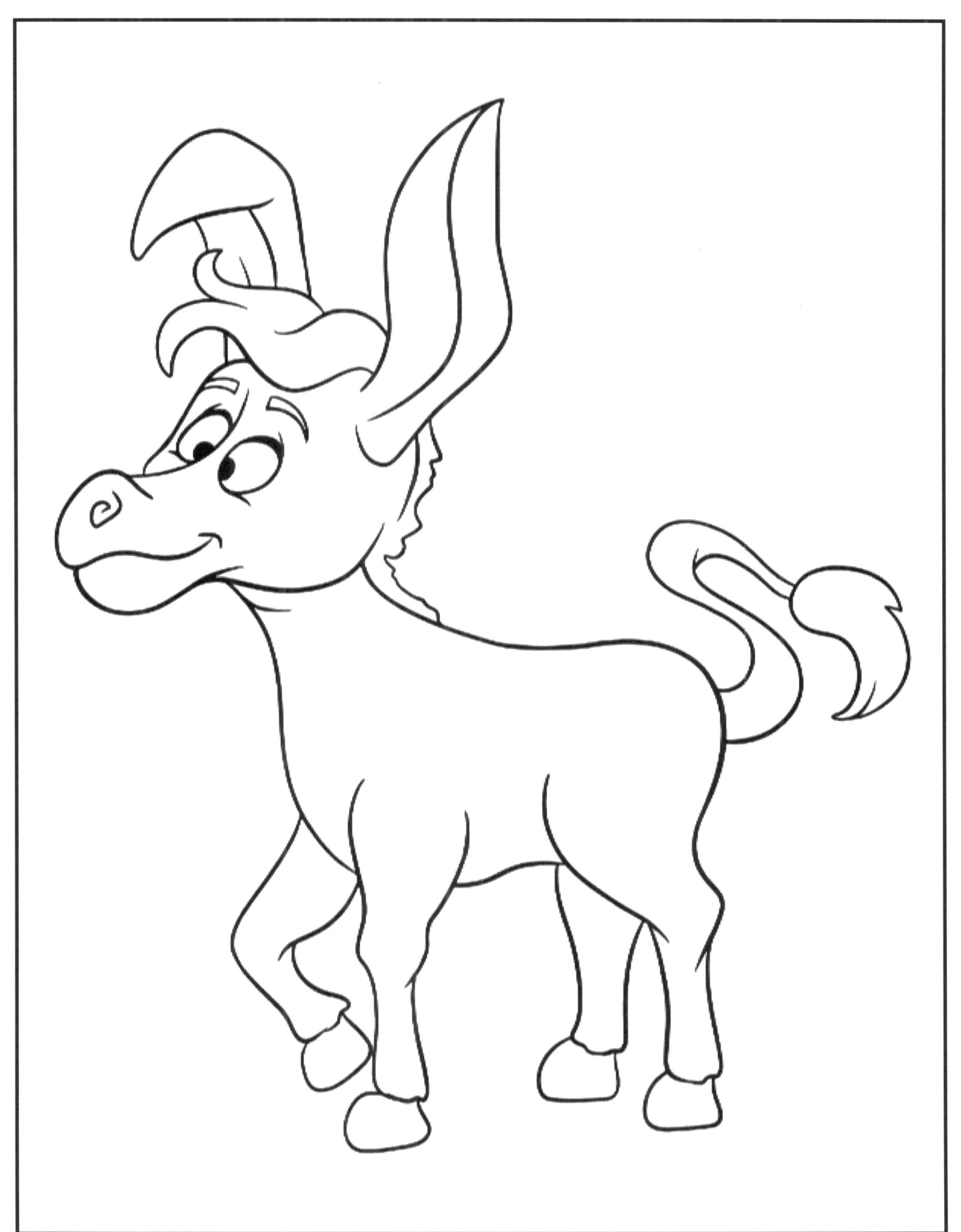

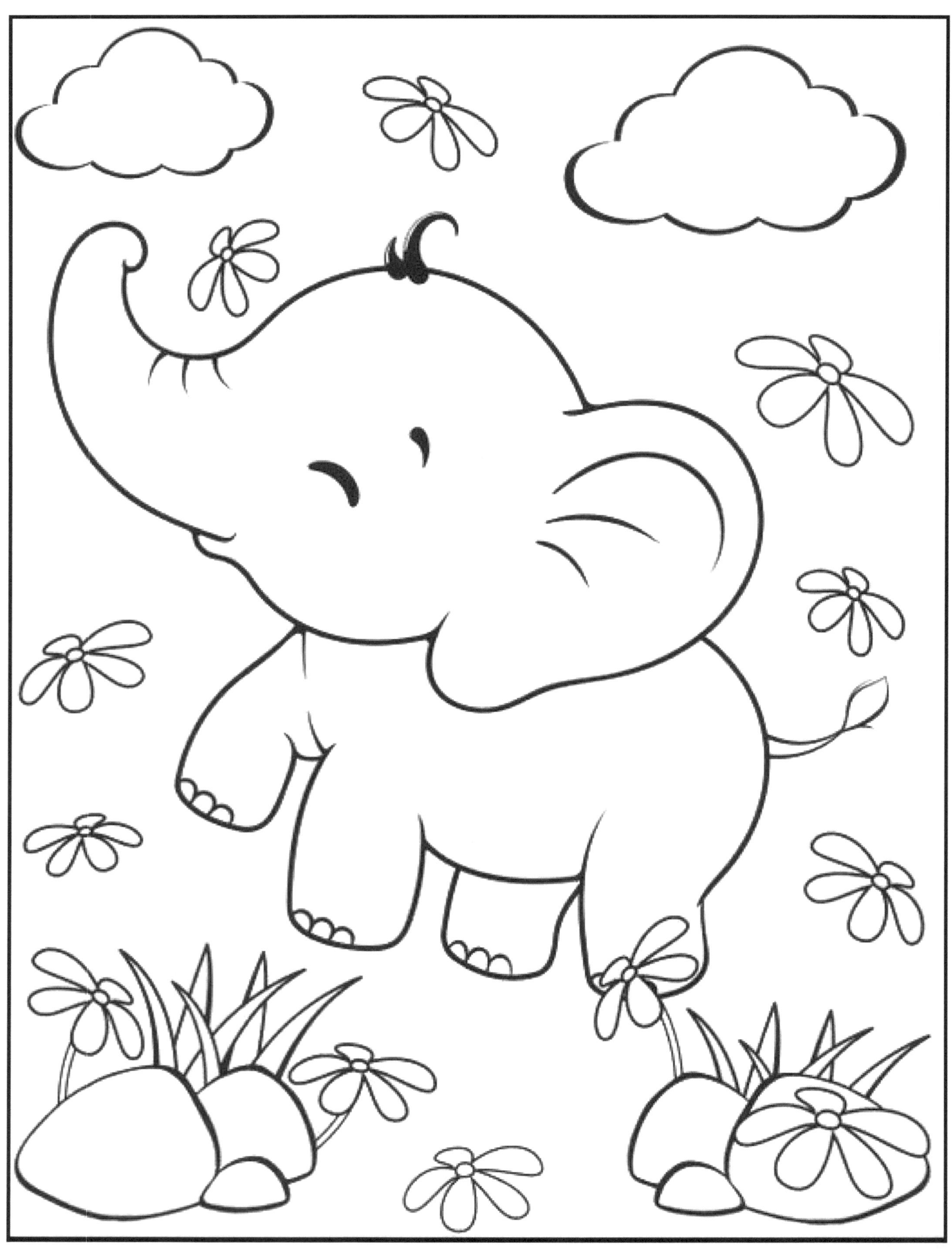

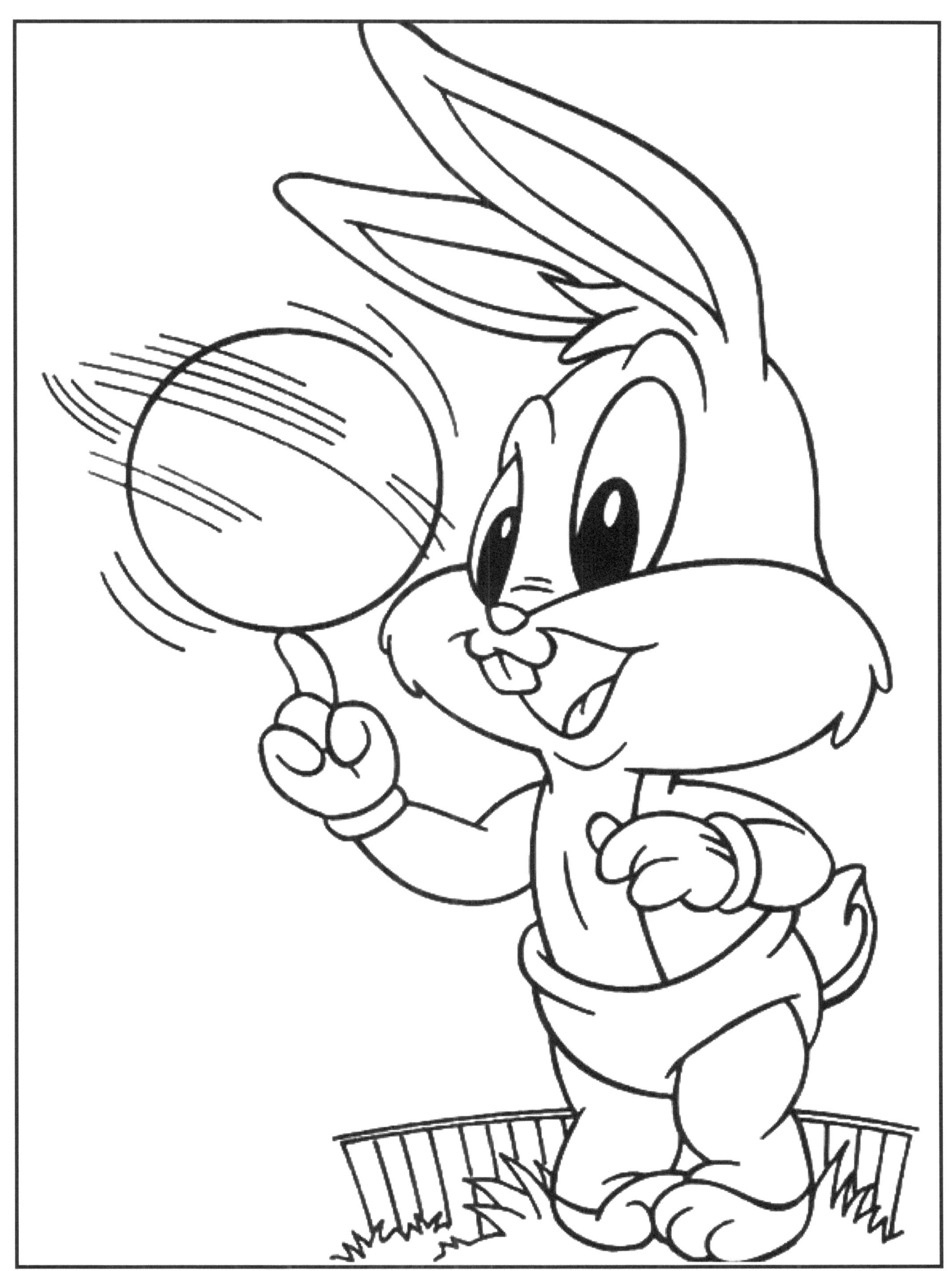

Play with colors

Notes

Notes

Notes

Notes

Notes

Notes